CHICAGO PUBLIC LIBRARY
SULZER REGIONAL
4455 N. LINCOLN
CHICAGO, IL 60625

SO-AZI-344

V/
87.4
35
2003

SULZER

JAN   2004

Exploring Canada

BRITISH COLUMBIA

Titles in the Exploring Canada series include:

Alberta

Manitoba

Ontario

Quebec

Yukon Territory

Exploring Canada

BRITISH
COLUMBIA

by Brett J. Palana

LUCENT
BOOKS®

THOMSON
★
TM
GALE

San Diego • Detroit • New York • San Francisco • Cleveland • New Haven, Conn. • Waterville, Maine • London • Munich

Development, management, design, and composition by Pre-Press Company, Inc.

© 2003 by Lucent Books. Lucent Books is an imprint of The Gale Group, Inc., a division of Thomson Learning, Inc.

Lucent Books® and Thomson Learning™ are trademarks used herein under license.

For more information, contact
Lucent Books
27500 Drake Rd.
Farmington Hills, MI 48331-3535
Or you can visit our Internet site at http://www.gale.com

ALL RIGHTS RESERVED.
No part of this work covered by the copyright hereon may be reproduced or used in any form or by any means—graphic, electronic, or mechanical, including photocopying, recording, taping, Web distribution or information storage retrieval systems—without the written permission of the publisher.

LIBRARY OF CONGRESS CATALOGING-IN-PUBLICATION DATA

Palana, B.J.
    British Columbia / by Brett J. Palana.
p. cm. — (Exploring Canada series)
Summary: Examines the history, geography, climate, industries, people, and culture of Canada's westernmost province.
Includes bibliographical references and index.
    ISBN 1-59018-046-1 (hardback : alk. paper)
    1. British Columbia—Juvenile literature. 2. British Columbia—History—Juvenile literature. [1. British Columbia. 2. Canada.] I. Title. II. Series.
    F1087.4 .P35 2003
    971.1—dc21
                                   2002004112

Printed in the United States of America

Contents

R0400541270

CHICAGO PUBLIC LIBRARY
SULZER REGIONAL
4455 N. LINCOLN
CHICAGO, IL 60625

Foreword

Any truly accurate portrait of Canada would have to be painted in sharp contrasts, for this is a long-inhabited but only recently settled land. It is a vast and expansive region peopled by a predominantly urban population. Canada is also a nation of natives and immigrants that, as its Prime Minister Lester Pearson remarked in the late 1960s, has "not yet found a Canadian soul except in time of war." Perhaps it is in these very contrasts that this elusive national identity is waiting to be found.

Canada as an inhabited place is among the oldest in the Western Hemisphere, having accepted prehistoric migrants more than eleven thousand years ago after they crossed a land bridge where the Bering Strait now separates Alaska from Siberia. Canada is also the site of the New World's earliest European settlement, L'Anse aux Meadows on the northern tip of Newfoundland Island. A band of Vikings lived there briefly some five hundred years before Columbus reached the West Indies in 1492.

Yet as a nation Canada is still a relative youngster on the world scene. It gained its independence almost a century after the American Revolution and half a century after the wave of nationalist uprisings in South America. Canada did not include Newfoundland until 1949 and could not amend its own constitution without approval from the British Parliament until 1982. "The Sleeping Giant," as Canada is sometimes known, came within a whisker of losing a province in 1995, when the people of Quebec narrowly voted down an independence referendum.

In 1999 Canada carved out a new territory, Nunavut, which has a population equal to that of Key West, Florida, spread over an area the size of Alaska and California combined.

As the second largest country in the world (after Russia), the land itself is also famously diverse. British Columbia's "Pocket Desert" near the town of Osoyoos is the northernmost desert in North America. A few hundred miles away, in Alberta's Banff National Park, one can walk on the Columbia Icefields, the largest nonpolar icecap in the world. In parts of Manitoba and the Yukon glacially created sand dunes creep slowly across the landscape. Quebec and Ontario have so many lakes in the boundless north that tens of thousands remain unnamed.

One can only marvel at a place where the contrasts range from the profound (the first medical use of insulin) to the mundane (the invention of Trivial Pursuit); the sublime (the poetry of Ontario-born Robertson Davies) to the ridiculous (the comic antics of Ontario-born Jim Carrey); the British (ever-so-quaint Victoria) to the French (Montreal, the world's second-largest French-speaking city); and the environmental (Greenpeace was founded in Vancouver) to the industrial (refuse from nickel mining near Sudbury, Ontario left a landscape so barren that American astronauts used it to train for their moon walks).

Given these contrasts and conflicts, can this national experiment known as Canada survive? Or to put it another way, what is it that unites as Canadians the elderly Inuit woman selling native crafts in the Yukon; the millionaire businessman-turned-restaurateur recently emigrated from Hong Kong to Vancouver; the mixed-French (Métis) teenager living in a rural settlement in Manitoba; the cosmopolitan French-speaking professor of archeology in Quebec City; and the raw-boned Nova Scotia fisherman struggling to make a living? These are questions only Canadians can answer, and perhaps will have to face for many decades.

A true portrait of Canada can't, therefore, be provided by a brief essay, any more than a snapshot captures the entire life of a centenarian. But the Exploring Canada Series can offer an illuminating overview of individual provinces and territories. Each book smartly summarizes an area's geography, history, arts and culture, daily life, and contemporary issues. Read individually or as a series, they show that what Canadians undeniably have in common is a shared heritage as people who came, whether in past millennia or last year, to a land with a difficult climate and a challenging geography, yet somehow survived and worked with one another to form a vibrant whole.

Gateway to the Pacific

B ritish Columbia is often called Canada's "Gateway to the Pacific," but "Gateway to the World" is how many British Columbians choose to view their unique province. British Columbia is the only province on Canada's west coast and therefore the only one with ports on the Pacific Ocean. Because of British Columbia's strategic location, the province has become Canada's link to the Asian "Pacific Rim" markets and to the U.S. West Coast markets as well. This has increased trade and made import and export businesses in British Columbia a dynamic segment of the economy. Other Canadian provinces wanting to participate in the Pacific Rim trade often ship their goods through British Columbia, thus boosting the economy of the already bustling region.

British Columbia earns much though not its entire livelihood from its global trade. Exports count as one-quarter of the gross domestic product with the natural resource industries being the leading source of this export revenue. This fact is no surprise as the lumber and mining industries thrive within the province and obtain more than half of their profits from exporting their goods to other countries. The United States accounts for 67 percent of British Columbia's total trade, and the Asian market accounts for 24 percent of British Columbia's exports. In addition, trade with Europe accounts for 7 percent of trade while trade with the other provinces of Canada accounts for only 6 percent of British Columbia's export revenue.

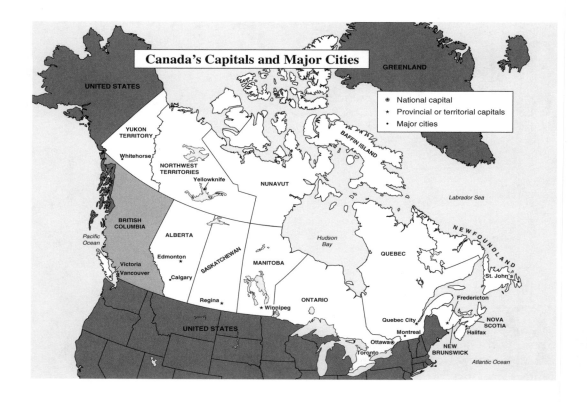

British Columbia's markets are so productive and profitable not only due to their high-quality products but also because of the province's location and trade conveniences. The majority of British Columbia's trade is with the United States on account of the fortunate circumstances of a shared time zone and low transportation costs. It takes only four hours for a product to leave Vancouver and arrive in Seattle, and less than a day for a product to reach San Francisco from Vancouver. In fact, British Columbia businesses can reach the entire western United States market within thirty-six hours. In addition to the timesaving benefits, trade between British Columbia and U.S. markets is duty-free (tax-free). All this spells convenience for the U.S. companies that do not have to worry about time differences or shipping overseas to conduct business.

Trade and shipping from British Columbia to the Asian market is also made more convenient and cost-efficient due to the province's location. Shipping goods from Vancouver to Asia can be a day or two faster than shipping the same load from Los Angeles. Another benefit British Columbia has in the Asian market is that Prince Rupert, the second busiest port in British Columbia, is the closest North American port to the thriving Asian market.

Yet the province does not merely rest on its fortunate location. It is working to make itself more attractive to foreign businesses both as a base for their operations and as a worthwhile investment opportunity. In the past ten years, thousands of highly skilled—and in many cases wealthy—immigrants and their families have made British Columbia their home. They have directly invested billions of dollars into business endeavors and in turn have created approximately seventy-five thousand jobs for British Columbians. The government of British Columbia is therefore eager to foster an attractive business climate.

The province is also diversifying its economy by focusing not only on its natural resources but also on its growing knowledge-based industries. British Columbia's spectacular mountain and coastal setting is another asset, attracting people from around the world to experience sailing, skiing, mountain biking, and numerous other recreational opportunities. In recent years the province has taken steps to improve its accessibility and transportation facilities and now offers a modern network of roads, railways, and air routes.

As a key player in the North American and international markets, British Columbia truly is a gateway to the Pacific

■ *The skyline of Vancouver, British Columbia's largest city and main commercial and cultural center.*

markets. The province, though connected to Canada politically and culturally, is in some respects an empire unto itself. With its bustling Pacific trade and the self-sufficiency it gains through its natural resource industry, British Columbia sometimes seems only loosely tied to Canada. One critic of the province commented that British Columbia is "divided from Canada by mountains, a desert, a moderate coastal climate, a time zone, and a general air of superiority."[1] Although this may be true, the people of British Columbia have worked hard to build their province into the thriving region it is today. British Columbia is very proud of its accomplishments, its position in the global market, and its individuality.

The Majestic West

B ritish Columbia gains much of its unique character and individuality from its unusual and varied environment. With weather that ranges from some of Canada's coldest to its wettest and warmest, British Columbia can offer its residents and visitors many adventures, from hiking through Canada's only true desert to ice climbing on alpine peaks. British Columbia contains regions so varied in terrain, climate, and plant and animal life that it almost seems an entire nation of its own. Here you'll find immense mountain ranges, the largest temperate rain forest in the world, and innumerable lakes and streams. Lava flows and fossil beds, a wider range of plant species than any other province, and Canada's only Pacific Ocean ports are also unique features of British Columbia. In addition, the province also encompasses thousands of Pacific Coast islands with their own unique character and rich diversity of land and sea features.

Massive and Mountainous

British Columbia is a huge and rugged land that covers 10 percent of Canada's total surface area. In shape, British Columbia looks somewhat like a bulked-up California, being longer than the state at some 1,000 miles (1,600 kilometers) north to south, and, at 450 miles (725 kilometers), about twice as wide. In fact, British Columbia is broad enough to need two time zones. British Columbia is Canada's third largest province, after Quebec and Ontario, but is larger than any state in the

13

■ *British Columbia's Fraser River begins in the Rocky Mountains and empties into the Pacific Ocean near Vancouver.*

United States with the exception of Alaska. British Columbia is larger than the states of California, Oregon, and Washington combined.

Over the past tens of millions of years much of British Columbia's land has been thrust upwards into mountain ranges. The province is Canada's most mountainous, with mountains occupying so much of the land that perhaps as little as 10 percent is suitable for grazing or agriculture. Two main mountain ranges, the Rocky Mountains that extend up its eastern edge and the Coast Mountains of the west, dominate British Columbia. Numerous smaller ranges, such as the Columbia Mountains in the south, ripple across the landscape and provide a backdrop to wide valleys.

The Canadian Rocky Mountains march into southern British Columbia from the area of its border with Washington, Idaho, and Montana. The Rockies form a spine up central and eastern British Columbia all the way into the Yukon and Northwest Territories. Along the province's eastern border, only in the far northeast corner do the mountains give way to the lowlands of Canada's Great Interior Plains. The Canadian Rockies feature rugged, snowcapped mountains and alpine glaciers. Mount Robson, at 12,972 feet (3,954 meters), on the British Columbia/Alberta border, is the highest peak of the Canadian Rockies.

The Canadian Rockies are part of the Rocky Mountains system that extends some 3,000 miles (4,800 kilometers) through North America, from New Mexico into Alaska. The Rockies divide the continent, causing rivers on the west side of the mountains to flow to the Pacific and those on the east to the Gulf of Mexico. Some of the river systems on the east side of the Rockies in central and northern British Columbia, such as the Peace and Liard (which originates in Yukon Territory), wind their way north through the Northwest Territories eventually to empty into the Arctic Ocean. The mountainous area in southeastern British Columbia, from Kootenay National Park to Jasper National Park, is where some of British Columbia's largest rivers, particularly the Fraser and Columbia, start their journey out of the Rockies bound for the Pacific. Rivers have played an important role in British Columbia, serving as routes through mountains for explorers and as sources of hydroelectric power (one of British Columbia's natural resources).

The Coast Mountains of British Columbia are nothing like the gentle coastal ranges found farther south on the continent. In fact the Coast Mountains are larger in total size and mass than Canada's Rockies—or any other mountain range in Canada. The Coast Mountains are rough and unforgiving, with many peaks that soar between 7,000 and 13,000 feet (2,100 to 3,900 meters). The highest point in the province, at 15,320 feet (4,670 meters), is at the top of the Coast Mountains' Mount Fairweather. The sixth-highest mountain in Canada, Fairweather sits in the far northwest section of British Columbia, on the border with Alaska and barely more than a dozen miles from the Pacific. Mount Fairweather is strangely named, since it gets some of the worst weather south of the Arctic. At the southern end of the Coast Mountains, where they merge with the northern end of the Cascade Range of western Washington and Oregon, high peaks hem in the population centers of Vancouver and Victoria. Active volcanoes (such as Washington's Mount St. Helens) and frequent earthquakes make the Cascades volatile—Vancouver Island was the site of Canada's largest onshore earthquake in 1946.

Between the Ranges

Mountains dominate much of mainland British Columbia but the area is also defined by its valleys, plateaus, lakes, and rivers. West of the Rocky Mountains, running north and south, lies a 1,000-mile (1,600-kilometer) trench that forms the longest

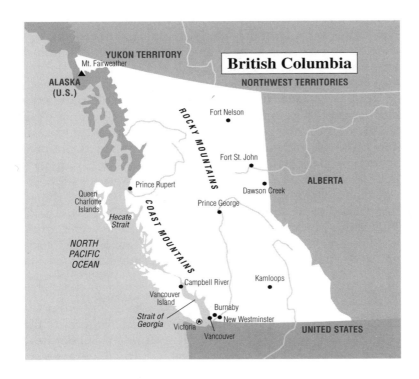

valley in North America. In addition, a wilderness highland (raised elevation) area, the Stikine Plateau in north-central British Columbia, lies between the province's great mountain ranges. Finally, there's the province's southern region, a mix of mountain ranges running north to south with deep valleys in between, creating much diversity in climate and geography.

The western boundary of the Rockies, all the way from Flathead Lake in Montana almost to the Yukon border, is a natural phenomenon known as the Rocky Mountain Trench. This interconnected chain of flat-bottomed valleys is so long (800 miles or 1,300 kilometers) that it can be spotted from space vehicles. The Trench is 3 to 8 miles wide (5 to 13 kilometers) and shows signs of glacial smoothing. Huge rivers like the Columbia have cut dramatic canyons at the Trench's edges. Exactly how the Trench was formed is still something of a mystery to geologists, with a likely theory pointing to the action of underground tectonic plates.

British Columbia's central high country is a rolling uplands region bordered by the Coast Mountains to the west and Rocky Mountain ranges, like the Cariboo, to the east. The vast forests and high alpine meadows are interspersed with cattle ranch lands, dry grasslands, and the occasional gold-mining-era ghost town, giving the area a wild-west flavor. The land south of the Stikine Plateau harbors many of the province's largest bodies of water, including T-shaped Williston Lake. This human-made reservoir, formed when the W.A.C. Bennett Dam was built on the Peace River in 1967 to generate hydroelectric power, is more than 120 miles (200 kilometers) long and has become a major recreational attraction in the area for its fishing, boating, and camping.

The southeast corner of British Columbia, a lowland situated between the Pacific Ocean and the Coast Mountains, is the location of the province's largest concentration of residents. The relatively mild summers and the many recreational attractions have also made southeastern British Columbia a popular tourist area. Okanagan Valley, the "sunny valley" located in the south-central area of British Columbia, is sheltered by the Cascade Mountain Range to the west and the Monashee Mountains on the east. It features orchards, lakes with sandy beaches, and vineyards. It is second to the Vancouver/Victoria area as the most populated area of British Columbia.

Rain Forest to Desert

The climate in British Columbia is influenced by the lay of the land, the flow of the ocean, and the waft of the wind. These three factors can produce an astonishing variation in temper-

ature and rainfall. Henderson Lake on Vancouver Island averages in excess of 250 inches (650 centimeters) of rain per year, making it the wettest place in North America, yet a desert exists within a few hundred miles!

■ *The plentiful rainfall near British Columbia's coasts allows the area's lush rain forest to thrive.*

Such extremes in rainfall are possible because of how clouds that form over the ocean are affected by coastal mountains. In the Northwest, air masses traveling over the Pacific pick up moisture. When clouds travel over the land and begin to gain elevation to pass over the Coast Mountains, they drop their load of rain. Once the clouds reach the opposite side of the mountains, they have only a limited supply of precipitation left. As a result, the coastal areas on the west side of the Coast Mountains receive relatively constant wet weather. Given the ample supply of precipitation, it is not surprising that British Columbia's rain forest exists in this area. Conversely, the interior of British Columbia just to the east of the Coast Mountains tends to be dry.

The many interior mountain ranges mean that climates in the same region can vary dramatically within small distances. But, in general, coastal British Columbia has a mild climate, with the central and northern interiors being more extreme. Northwestern British Columbia tends to have snowy winters and short, cool, and wet summers. The southwestern corner experiences the province's mildest weather and fewest extremes. Temperatures in Vancouver average in the 70s F (21° to 26° C) during the summer and in the 30s F (−1° to 4° C) during the winter. Rain is more prevalent during winter than snow.

British Columbia's southern interior valleys can get very hot summer weather when warm fronts move up from the continental United States. The seasonal weather here varies greatly depending upon the valley. The Okanagan Valley region is protected from the cool sea air by the Coast Mountains, and as a result, has a dry, warm climate—summer temperatures average close to 80° F (27° C) and may soar beyond 90° F (32° C). To the east, the Kootenay region is cooler and wetter, with snow-dusted mountains even in the summer.

Northeastern and north-central British Columbia are more affected by cold air masses sweeping down from the polar regions than by the moderate air masses from the Pacific. The interior plateau region experiences dry weather with long, bone-chilling winters. The summers are short but warm enough to sustain some agriculture, especially grains and forage crops such as hay for livestock. Extended spells with little rain, however, prevent farmers from growing many vegetable crops—most parts of the central plateau receive only 15 to 20 inches (38 to 51 centimeters) of rain annually, about what California averages from San Francisco to Los Angeles.

■ British Columbia's Pocket Desert

At the southern tip of the Okanagan Valley, a few miles from the Washington State border, lies one of the northernmost deserts in the world. People in the nearby town of Osoyoos (o-sue-use) call it their "Pocket Desert," tucked as it is between the surrounding highlands, a lower valley (much of which is irrigated for vineyards and orchards), and Lake Osoyoos. Canada's only desert is actually an extension of the great Sonoran desert of North America, parts of which stretch all the way from New Mexico.

The local geography and arid climate created the desert. Close in to the eastern side of the Coast Mountains, the area receives little moisture from the rain-depleted clouds that venture over the range. The hot and dry summers, mild winters, and the well-drained, sandy soil have created a desert dominated by sparse, drought-resistant grasses and plants, such as antelope-brush, various species of sagebrush, prickly pear cactus, and primitive-looking smooth scouring rush. The animal life is also unusual for Canada: pocket gophers, quail, western rattlesnake, and coyote share the demanding environment. In many cases the plant and animal life is rare or endangered. The Pocket Desert is not big, and animals adapted to its unique ecosystems may not survive anywhere else in Canada, or even the world. Rare animals include the tiger salamander, sage thrasher, night snake, nuttall's cottontail, great basin spadefoot toad, and wind scorpion. The Pocket Desert now attracts many visitors, and steps have been taken in recent years to protect this unique and fragile environment.

In addition to the wide and varying landscapes of the mainland, British Columbia also contains an abundance of islands each unique in its own right.

A Land of Many Islands

British Columbia's massive mainland is complemented by some sixty-five hundred coastal islands. These range from huge and populous Vancouver Island in the south to the isolated Queen Charlotte archipelago in the north, just below the Alaskan panhandle. The island way of life—ferries, boating, fishing—is an integral part of the British Columbia identity.

■ *A ferry makes its way to Vancouver Island. Ferries are a fixture of British Columbia's many waterways.*

Bigger than Vermont, Vancouver Island stretches 285 miles (460 kilometers) in length and 30 to 80 miles (50 to 130 kilometers) in width. Its overall area of more than 12,400 square miles (32,000 square kilometers) makes it the largest island off the west coast of North America. The west coast of Vancouver Island is a mostly uninhabited, forested, and roadless area of deep fjords and coastal mountains. It receives more rain and snow than anywhere else in North America. The eastern side of the island consists of low-lying lands more favorable to human habitation: 97 percent of the island's population lives within the area that extends from the capital city of Victoria in the south to the city of Campbell River halfway up the east coast. Vancouver Island is tucked in close to the mainland but not close enough for any bridges—this is an area of ferries. The province's largest city, Vancouver, is not on Vancouver Island but rather across the broad Strait of Georgia on the mainland.

The Strait of Georgia was once known as the Gulf of Georgia, which is why the islands there are called the Gulf Islands. (The misnaming was the fault of the British explorer George Vancouver, who in the early 1790s was the first European to sail around the island. Upon reaching the southern tip of the island, he mistook what was later proven to be a strait for a gulf.) Hundreds of islands dot the strait. The dozen main Gulf Islands, lying close in to the protective shelter of Vancouver Island's southeast coast, have a mild, often sunny climate similar to countries along the Mediterranean. Many

Gulf Islands contain scenic beaches, pasturelands, and forests. Salt Spring is the largest and most developed island and Mayne the most pastoral.

Close to the mainland and blessed with a favorable climate, Vancouver Island and the Gulf Islands are prime residential areas of British Columbia. Farther north, and farther out to sea, the Queen Charlotte Islands show the wilder, more remote side of British Columbia's island identity.

The Isolated Queen Charlotte Islands

The Queen Charlotte Islands include two large islands, Graham (which is larger than the province of Prince Edward Island) and Moresby, and 150 additional islands. They are all much more distant from the mainland compared to Vancouver Island and the Gulf Islands. Access is by ferry, across the choppy, 80-mile-wide (130-kilometer-wide) Hecate Strait, or by plane. These islands' remote location left them unaffected by the continental glaciers that covered the rest of British Columbia numerous times over the past 2 million years. The isolation and lack of glaciation combined to create an ecology on the Queen Charlotte Islands that is unique in Canada:

> The timber supply area is part of a large and complex island ecological system. Animals unique to the area include a sub-species of North American black bear, a sub-species of pine marten (both larger than their mainland cousins), and species of deer mouse, dusky shrew, and short-tailed weasel. Concerns over the population decline of the Queen Charlotte goshawk and marbled murrelet prompted their listing as . . . threatened and endangered species. Sitka black-tailed deer, raccoons, squirrels, beaver, and three species of rats were introduced to the islands and now exist in great numbers—much to the detriment of some native plants and animals.[2]

Unfortunately, logging has reduced much of the lush rain forest once abundant on Graham and northwest Moresby. In 1988 the government of Canada and the native Haida (a First Nations culture that has survived on the Queen Charlotte Islands since well before European settlement) began to protect some of the remaining rain forest, as well as abandoned Haida villages, by setting aside South Moresby Island as the Gwaii Haanas ("place of wonder" in the language of the Haida) National Park Reserve. Parks and preserves now account for more than one-fifth of the islands' land.

The Queen Charlotte Islands are only sparsely populated, with approximately one-third of the population of six thousand residents being Haida. Although much of the culture and tradition of the Haida failed to survive conflict with the

■ The Inside Passage

British Columbia's Inside Passage is a spectacular coastal water route from Port Hardy on the northern tip of Vancouver Island to Prince Rupert, near Canada's border with Alaska. This sheltered, 300-mile (490-kilometer) marine highway is part of the longer coastal waterway that extends from Victoria up into the Alaskan panhandle, following a series of natural channels between the numerous protective islands and the mainland. In the past, mainly fishing vessels and local sailors plied British Columbia's Inside Passage. Today, however, tour boats and even cruise ships make stately, fifteen-hour journeys. The Inside Passage is also known as a world-class sea kayak route. The trip up or down the Inside Passage is breathtakingly beautiful as it travels past towering, densely wooded mountains, steep-walled fjords, narrow gorges, and other magnificent natural wonders of British Columbia.

■ *Kayakers paddle through the spectacular Inside Passage off Vancouver Island.*

Europeans, the intricately carved and designed totem poles found on the islands have helped to uncover some of the fascinating history and accomplishments of the Haida people.

A Province of Trees

Whether on mainland or island, British Columbia is inseparable from its forests. "The outstanding feature of this province is its trees,"[3] according to ecologist Ivan T. Sanderson. Forests cover two-thirds of British Columbia, so it is no surprise that the province is famous for its trees and produces 40 percent of Canada's commercial wood. The greatest numbers of the trees that crowd the interior of the province are conifers such as Douglas fir, western white and lodgepole pines, and Sitka spruce. The most luxuriant forests of British Columbia, however, grow along the coast. It is here that the mild, wet climate, influenced by Pacific coastal currents, produces some of the largest trees and most dense foliage in the world.

The coastal temperate rain forest along British Columbia's Pacific coast is one of the largest in the world. (Coastal rain forests are so rare that they cover only about 2 percent of the earth's total surface.) At the top of the rain forest are the crowns of giant conifers, such as Douglas fir and western hemlock. In the understory you find smaller conifers and hardwoods such as aspens, alders, and birches. On the floor is a distinct and vibrant layer, a dense carpet of ferns, mosses, lichens, bushes, and flowers all jumbled up with the fallen and rotting logs and branches from the upper layers. A simple walk in the woods can present problems:

> The floor of this forest is often hard to find, being feet below the apparent surface, and in virgin areas you have to be extremely careful or you may break through the mat of mosses, ferns, dead branches, and general tangle and drop down into a tridimensional latticework of fallen and rotting tree trunks below. A companion of mine once so vanished instantly, right before my eyes, and I had to fetch a rope to get him out, for he was wedged between two great logs about ten feet down in a sort of cave with overhanging sides formed by a crisscross of age-old rotting logs.[4]

The southern coast of British Columbia is also the home of numerous beautifully flowering trees such as the Oregon crabapple and the Pacific dogwood, British Columbia's provincial tree. The dogwood thrives in the deep, well-drained soil of the coastal mainland regions as well as on the coast of Vancouver Island. The plant grows as either a shrub or a small tree and

■ *Kootenay National Park, home to some of the province's many beautiful forests.*

■ The Mighty Douglas Firs

In the Pacific Northwest, with its humid climate and fertile soil, the Douglas fir has thrived. The conifer is now one of the most common trees in British Columbia and is the leading timber-producing tree in North America. It is also one of the hardiest, largest, and most long-lived trees on the earth. Its fire-resistant bark can grow up to a foot thick. A Douglas fir can attain a remarkable 380 feet (115 meters) in height and in exceptional cases live longer than a millennium.

The botanical name of the genus is *Pseudotsuga*, which means false (pseudo) hemlock (tsuga), because of its resemblance to hemlocks. Among the six species, only two are native to North America and the one in particular (*Pseudotsuga menziesii*) that grows in the Pacific Northwest is referred to as the Douglas fir. The popular name honors the early-nineteenth-century Scottish botanist David Douglas, who traveled thousands of miles along the coast of the Pacific Northwest observing plants and collecting specimens. Around 1825 he was astonished to see this mighty evergreen tree.

The most common use for the Douglas fir, aside from the long and straight trunks being logged for lumber, relates to its position as a holiday centerpiece: Douglas firs are the most popular Christmas trees in both the United States and Canada. Douglas firs play a much more important role, however, in the ecology of northern forests. Because of the trees' thick bark, they can resist low-intensity forest fires, over time leading to a forest with a diverse mixture of young and old trees. Douglas fir forests also provide an excellent winter habitat for animals such as white-tailed deer and Rocky Mountain elk.

■ *The hardy, fire-resistant Douglas fir tree dominates British Columbia's landscape.*

reaches about 45 feet (15 meters) in height. The dogwood yields white flowers, which are actually four to six leaves, and elongated dark red berries that attract bears, beavers, and birds. Because the Pacific dogwood is the floral emblem of British Columbia, it is illegal to move or cut down one in the wild.

An Animal Paradise

British Columbia's varying plant life, in combination with its diverse geography and climate, has created abundant opportunities for animals to thrive. Large mammals like the grizzly bear and moose share the province with tiny sea otters and mink. Coastal rain forests harbor a variety of birds, ground animals, and frogs and other amphibians, while you might find horned lizards and eastern rattlesnakes in parts of the southern interior. The coastal islands and surrounding waters are chock full of sea birds, while the fish of British Columbia are the most abundant in Canada.

British Columbia's many wild and remote areas have allowed large mammals to thrive. Packs of wild timber wolves hunt in the forests of the mainland. The grassy areas around rivers and streams are perfect for bears to feed on berries, roots, and fish. British Columbia contains almost one-quarter of Canada's black bears and half of its grizzlies. The many rocky crags and rough slopes of the interior mountains offer a home to agile bighorn sheep and mountain goats. Vancouver Island contains the largest population of cougars in North America. Other large animals native to British Columbia include Roosevelt and Rocky Mountain elk; three species of deer; and moose and caribou.

Wildlife is abundant in the sea as well as on the land in British Columbia. The waters of British Columbia are rich in herring, trout, pike, shellfish, and many other kinds of fish. The size and variety of salmon are legendary—there's the bright red sockeye, the monster-sized king or chinook, and the silvery coho. British Columbia's fishing industry is the largest of any Canadian province. In addition to fish, the Pacific coast supports a pair of unusual sea mammals, the sea otter and the killer whale, that may need British Columbia as a final refuge from extinction.

Threatened Sea Otters

At a length of only three to four feet (one meter plus), sea otters are the second smallest mammal in the ocean, after the South American marine otter. The playful sea otter is native to the ocean waters of the Pacific, from California up to Alaska and around the Aleutians to Russia. Sea otters spend almost all of their life in the water. Large groups are called "rafts" and may include several hundred animals segregated by sex. Individuals sometimes rest at sea by wrapping themselves in strands of kelp, a seaweed. Sea otters are one of the few marine mammals known to use tools—they use rocks or other objects to pound or pry open the shells of crabs, clams, and abalones (a mollusk that clings to rocks).

Sea otters do not have the thick layer of blubber that keeps other sea animals like the whale and the seal warm in the cold ocean waters. Instead, sea otters have the thickest fur coat of any mammal. A single individual has an estimated 800 million hairs, averaging a million hairs per square inch. In contrast, a dog has only 60,000 hairs per square inch, and a human has only 100,000 hairs in total.

■ *British Columbia's sea otter population has recovered after nearly going extinct.*

The thickness and softness of their pelts made sea otters a prized fur in the eighteenth and nineteenth centuries. By the early twentieth century the animal had been hunted to near extinction, with its total population perhaps as low as two thousand individuals. In recent years it has been protected as an endangered species by both the Canadian and U.S. governments and has recovered in numbers, with perhaps fifty thousand alive today.

Two new threats to sea otters, however, have surfaced in recent years: oil-polluted waters and predation from killer whales. Oil mats otters' fur and prevents the formation of the insulating air space that usually exists between the fur and the cold water. Without the air space, sea otters can freeze to death. Because sea otters constantly preen their fur, they can also ingest the toxic oil. For these reasons, the sea otter fatality rate is very high in offshore oil spills.

Killer Whales on the Loose

Until recently killer whales weren't much of a threat to sea otters, preferring larger prey such as Stellar's sea lions. Because large numbers of sea lions have been killed in fishermen's nets, however, the distinctively patterned, black-and-white killer whales are now forced to eat sea otters. Like the sea otter, killer whales are more abundant in British Columbia than perhaps anywhere else in the world. An estimated three hundred reside year-round in the waters of British Columbia.

One of the best places to observe concentrations of these marine mammals is the Johnstone Strait off the northern tip of Vancouver Island. During the spring and summer, pods (groups of five to ten animals) of killer whales gather here to feast on the migrating salmon. They also engage in their entertaining breaching (jumping out of the water), tail slapping, and spyhopping (coming partially out of the water, apparently to get a better look at something, like an approaching boat). Some pods also do beach rubbing: massaging their bodies on the smooth, flat pebbles near the shore. British Columbia is one of the few places in the world where anyone has seen a killer whale giving birth in the wild.

Killer whales, also known as orcas, are the largest member of the dolphin family. Males may grow to 30 feet (10 meters) and weigh in at ten tons. They were given their ferocious name because they are the only member of the cetacean (whale) order that regularly eats birds and other mammals. They are highly social (pods seem to be part of a larger clan that may travel together) and apparently talkative—they use calls to communicate.

A New Focus on Conservation

British Columbia prizes its plants and animals, its wilderness and its natural resources, its forests and coastal waters, with just cause. Its vast expanses of trees, unique temperate rain forest, and rivers and bays teeming with fish are natural resources that have long supported much of the province's economy:

> Superabundant natural resources in ocean, rivers, and forests helped Northwestern natives achieve an unusually high standard of material culture long before the arrival of Europeans, drawn here by this same natural bounty. The fur traders were the first to come, followed by mineral prospectors, fishermen, ranchers, and lumbermen. Today's provincial economy still depends largely on the exploitation of what were once seen as almost limitless resources.[5]

■ *An orca, or killer whale, sprays mist from its blowhole as it travels with a pod.*

■ Mysterious Creatures

Some of British Columbia's wildlife is so mysterious—or perhaps mythic—that it has never been documented. Such is the case with a sea serpent said to live in the depths of 90-mile (145-kilometer) -long Lake Okanagan in south-central British Columbia. The creature is popularly known as Ogopogo, or N'ha-a-itk ("lake demon") by the local Indians. Native legends tell of animal sacrifices made to appease the monster so parties would not be attacked as they crossed the waters. Like Scotland's Loch Ness monster "Nessie," Ogopogo is usually described as a long serpentlike creature with humps on its back and a large head. An early story of Ogopogo tells of two horses swimming across the lake tied to their owner's boat. Without warning the horses were mysteriously pulled beneath the waters. The owner of the horses is said to have survived only by cutting the rope that attached the horses. More recent tales of Ogopogo tend to portray a tame creature merely interested in feeding on fish or weeds.

Like Nessie, Ogopogo's existence has never been scientifically verified. In both cases believers point to the extreme depths of the bodies of water (Lake Okanagan is almost 1,000 feet deep in some parts) as a reason for believing a population of large animals could remain unknown to humans. In a final parallel with Nessie, Ogopogo in recent years has been transformed from monster to regional pet, referred to with whimsy rather than fear and displayed proudly on local T-shirts, postcards, and restaurant menus. There's even a cartoonish Ogopogo statue in Kelowna's City Park.

An even more famous mystery monster of British Columbia is Sasquatch or Bigfoot, the North American version of the Himalayan's Abominable Snowman. Sasquatch is said to be a hairy, larger-than-human, apelike creature that survives in remote mountain forests and communicates through birdlike whistles. The evidence for the creature's existence, such as large tracks left in snow, is inconclusive and most scientists are skeptical or dismissive. The myth of Sasquatch, however, has become a part of British Columbia's wildlife lore.

■ *A statue of Sasquatch, or Bigfoot, in British Columbia.*

■ *British Columbians protest the deforestation of old growth trees by the timber industry.*

Yet, in recent years, many people have begun to question the way some of these provincial treasures had been exploited. Huge swaths of Vancouver Island were clear-cut of its primeval forest. The salmon at Salmon Arm in Shuswap Lake in south-central British Columbia were considered so abundant they were plucked from the water and spread on the ground as fertilizer.

Many British Columbians have reacted with anger and sadness over such exploitation and waste. The province has become a focal point for environmental action, and was the birthplace of the now international-in-scope Greenpeace group. The provincial government recognized the need for "protection, conservation, and management of provincial wildlife, water, land, and air resources . . . and the protection and management of provincial parks, recreation areas, and ecological reserves"[6] and formed the Ministry of Environment, Lands and Parks. British Columbia now boasts some 675 parks and reserves and has devoted to wilderness more than 11 percent of its area. But the task is not an easy one. Logging and other natural-resource-based industries are responsible for considerable employment and tax revenue for the province.

The province's varied climate and diverse landscape contribute to its individuality and its mind-set of independence. In many ways, British Columbia is unlike the rest of Canada, focused as it is on the Pacific and the ways the ocean influences its weather, agriculture, society, and economy. British Columbia has long been a unique empire, and its people continue to view it as such.

The First Nations, the First Europeans, and the Companies

British Columbia is home to people of many cultures and traditions, and this has been true since well before the area became a Canadian province. Asian hunters and gatherers, having crossed the Bering Strait during the Ice Age, were the original residents of British Columbia, and Chinese or Japanese fishermen who plied the waters of the Pacific may have touched ashore before the Europeans. The list of nationalities that later immigrated to British Columbia is as diverse as the land itself. Of the many people who have had a great impact on the future of British Columbia through their culture, their discoveries, and their landholdings, three are the most significant: the First Nations, the European explorers, and the employees of the Hudson's Bay and North West Companies. British Columbia would not be the place it is today without the influence of these three groups.

The First Nations

The native peoples of British Columbia collectively call themselves the First Nations. When Europeans first began to settle in British Columbia in the early 1800s, an estimated 200,000 native peoples lived in the region from the Aleutians to present-day northern California. Historians surmise that some of these groups had occupied the region for over ten thousand years, and possibly much longer. During that time the abundant natural resources in the area, and the moderate climate along the coast, allowed them to develop complex societies

■ *An illustration from Captain Cook's voyage in the Nootka Sound shows the homes and boats of Vancouver Island's native people.*

with prosperous economies, distinct languages, and sophisticated arts and crafts.

These native societies differed somewhat depending on their location. The native peoples of the coastal areas, such as the Nootka, Haida, and the Coast Salish, were known for their skills at both trading and fishing, and the two occupations often supported each other. These native tribes benefited from the abundant supply of salmon and other fish in the coastal and lower river regions. Coastal tribes lived in permanent settlements, usually rectangular communal lodges made of wood. Their clothing was made from cedar and other barks, or from sea otter, bear, or other animal fur.

Inland tribes like the Kootenay, the Beaver, and the Carrier, on the other hand, had a harder time gaining a sufficient supply of salmon, as the sockeye was the only species that would fight its way upstream into the major inland waterways. During the years when the sockeye stock was diminished, the inland tribes would suffer. As a result, the inland tribes developed a greater dependence on hunting animals such as mountain goats, bear, and beaver than their coastal counterparts. The tribes of the interior also were nomadic societies that moved from place to place depending on the season and the availability of food.

Complex and Successful Societies

Despite their differences, the native people of the Pacific Northwest shared similarities in customs, social organization, ceremonies, and other aspects. Most First Nations tribes were made up of closely knit groups of related families, or lineages,

■ The Haida

The Haida are a First Nations tribe residing primarily on the Queen Charlotte Islands off British Columbia's northwest coast and also, to a lesser degree, across the Dixon Entrance strait on the southern end of Alaska's Prince of Wales Island. The Haida were expert fishermen and sailors and were able to harvest sea species as well as freshwater fish like salmon. The Haida were also renowned for their woodcarving skills. They built complex cedar plank houses, which oftentimes were multifamily and multilevel. In addition, the canoes built by them were some of the largest and most ornately decorated of the Canadian tribes. The Haida's intricately carved totems represented a family's pride in its ancestry. The creatures (which were both mystical and natural) on the poles were specific to each family. The poles would often serve as memorials to deceased members of the tribe or as portal poles to the afterlife.

The Haida Society was originally divided into two clans, the Raven and the Eagle clans, and marriage was always with someone of the opposite clan. One's clan was assigned matrilinearly (through the mother's family). Therefore, when a couple wed, they and their future children would become members of the bride's clan. Each clan would exist as its own separate unit for both landowning and ceremonial practices, and each would be led by its own hereditary chief.

In the early eighteenth century, there were approximately eight thousand Haida, but by 1880 diseases, particularly smallpox and venereal infections, brought by the European fur traders reduced the population to two thousand. During this dramatic population decline, the Queen Charlotte Island survivors gathered in multiclan villages, two of which remain, Masset and Skidegate. Today, many of the Haida have left the Queen Charlotte Islands to pursue opportunities on the mainland, and some of the remaining Haida guide tourists through the islands they once dominated.

that would live in large wooden winter houses or a cluster of houses in a village. To assign social rank, people were divided into three classes (nobility, commoners, and slaves) depending primarily upon ancestry. The commoners made up the largest part of the population. The slaves were generally captives or descendants of captives. As with any system of rank, certain privileges accompanied each class. For instance, the right to decorate oneself or one's home with certain symbols was determined by rank.

The First Nations tribes of British Columbia formed complex societies with intricate dynamics of family, rank, and wealth. Despite their long history of life in the Northwest, the tribes ultimately were suppressed by the massive influx of European settlers who infiltrated the First Nations' lands and claimed them as their own.

■ The Potlatch

An important social custom that many native cultures of the coastal regions shared was the *potlatch,* derived from a Nootka word referring to a type of ceremonial feast. The earliest potlatches probably celebrated events such as a successful hunt. The tribe would gather around the food and offer thanks and honor to the chief. Eventually families began to organize potlatches to celebrate births, weddings, and even deaths. The head of the family would offer gifts to the guests, such as blankets or food. In addition to the gift giving, potlatches would include speeches, singing, dancing, and feasting. The speech was considered the privilege of the host, and in it he asserted his ancestral privileges and his status in the community. Masks and headdresses would be worn in the dances to celebrate the host's deceased relatives or the host himself.

Potlatches were normally held in the winter months, and though they acted as a celebration, they were also a way owner-

■ *A photo from the early 1900s of a potlatch in Duncan, British Columbia.*

The Early Europeans

European exploration of the Pacific Northwest had begun slowly, and many explorers simply stumbled upon the area in search of other destinations. Such was the case in 1592 when Spanish sailor Juan de Fuca left Mexico to find a sea passage from the Pacific to the Atlantic. De Fuca did not find the passage he sought, but he did chart on his maps a deep strait opening into a broad gulf, which he hoped would lead to the Atlantic. Of course, the mainland of what would become British Columbia, not to mention the rest of North America, separated his bay from the Atlantic, and de Fuca soon gave up and returned south. The Strait of Juan de Fuca, between the southern tip of Vancouver Island and Washington State, still bears his name. In 1774, the Spanish again sailed to the coast of British Columbia, this time led by Juan Perez. These explorations did not lead to any Spanish settlements, but Spain still claimed the area as part of its empire.

ship, heritage, and economic privileges were asserted, displayed, and passed on. The potlatch acted as a political system for the tribes and certainly as an identifier of societal rank. Commoners' potlatch ceremonies were attended mainly by fellow tribal people, whereas elites often invited guests from other tribes. One's place at the potlatch also indicated rank. Highly esteemed members of society were seated at the best locations and were always served food first, in any amount they desired.

When the Europeans arrived in the Pacific Northwest with their array of new material goods, potlatches became less about dancing and feasting and more about giving gifts and displaying wealth. Potlatches would be elaborate affairs lasting several days. The host of the potlatch would shower guests with valuable gifts, including furs, canoes, slaves, jewelry, precious metals, and totems. The generosity was a sign of the host's wealth and position in society. Guests would be expected to match or exceed these gifts when they themselves held a potlatch for an event in their own family. In some cases the host of a potlatch would demonstrate his wealth and status by actually destroying his valuables! In some tribes, the potlatch became a harmful competition in which members would bankrupt themselves to outdo each other.

Today, some First Nations peoples still hold potlatches. Ceremonies typically last for up to a day, unlike the weeklong festivals of the past, but may commit the host family to feeding and entertaining several hundred invited guests. Hosts also still offer gifts, including cash, to guests.

The British were the next to arrive when the famous globetrotter Captain James Cook sailed up from the South Pacific in 1778. Cook had a Russian map that displayed a northwest passage between Alaska and the land to the south. Cook believed that if he followed de Fuca's strait north, he would encounter the passage, so he set out to investigate the strait. Cook's ship, however, was blown off course and ended up in what came to be known as the Nootka Sound on the west coast of the large island. Cook and his crew went ashore, unsure of what they would find. To the Europeans' relief, the natives were friendly and eager to trade their furs for British goods. Cook and his men left the area with ships full of furs to bring back to Europe.

Cook himself never made it back to Europe—he was killed by natives in Hawaii on his return—but news of his successful fur trading in the Pacific Northwest created excitement among British merchants. By 1788 a British explorer, John Meares, had set up a trading post on the large island to ship sea otter furs to China. In 1789, however, the Spanish

seized the post. Britain and Spain were nearly ready to declare war over the disputed area, but instead they signed the Nootka Convention in 1790. This treaty granted equal rights to traders from both countries.

The Spanish then sent explorer Don Juan Quadra to explore and map the area, while the British sent ships under the command of George Vancouver. In 1792 Vancouver entered the Strait of Juan de Fuca and sailed around the island that would one day bear his name. The coastal charts Vancouver compiled from 1792 to 1794 are the first records of the islands and inlets of the area.

■ *Captain James Cook's exploration in the Nootka Sound opened up the area to British trade.*

Mackenzie's Search for an Overland Route

Shortly after Vancouver arrived in British Columbia by sea, a party led by the Canadian fur trader and explorer Alexander Mackenzie arrived by land. Mackenzie's journey, after years of planning and one notable false start, would eventually open the way for thousands more. Prior to Mackenzie, no Europeans had made an overland crossing of North America north of Mexico.

Mackenzie was born in Scotland in 1764. His mother died while he was still young, so he traveled with his father to New York. Once there, Mackenzie was raised by his two aunts until the age of fifteen, when he was sent to Montreal to apprentice in a fur-trading firm. By 1787 he had become a partner in one of the companies that merged to form the North West Company, the trading firm that came to rival the Hudson's Bay Company.

In 1788 Mackenzie was posted to Fort Chipewyan on Lake Athabasca (in what is now northern Alberta and Saskatchewan) to supervise North West's fur trade in the district. There he met Peter Pond, who introduced Mackenzie to his theory of a river route to the Pacific. Pond believed that two great rivers connected Great Slave Lake to the Pacific. Great Slave Lake, in what is now Northwest Territories, lies north of Lake Athabasca but is connected by the Slave River. Pond figured that it might take only six days of paddling west on one of these routes to reach the ocean. Pond was, of course, badly mistaken in his geography (both of his great rivers were on the wrong side of the continental divide to reach the Pacific) and distance (even if you could paddle to the Pacific, it would surely take more like sixty than six days), as Mackenzie would find out for himself over the next five years.

From the Peace to the Pacific

Four years after his disappointing trip to the Arctic, Mackenzie tried again. In May 1793 he launched another expedition to find the river route to the Pacific—this time following Pond's second great river, the Peace. When the river narrowed and turned to rapids, Mackenzie and his men were forced to climb the surrounding cliffs. The expedition continued by land, at times advancing only a few miles a day as the men hacked their way through thick forest, sleeping where they fell from exhaustion. Native tribes, including the Sekani and the Carrier, helped and guided Mackenzie and his crew several times along the way.

On May 14, 1793, the expedition crossed the continental divide in present-day north-central British Columbia and became the first Europeans to explore mainland British Columbia. The group ultimately found its way to what Mackenzie thought to be the upper reaches of the Columbia River (it was actually what was later to be named the Fraser River). Heading overland again, they reached and crossed the Coast Mountains and entered the coastal rain forest. There they were greeted by the Bella Coola Indians, a friendly tribe that fed the explorers and gave them a new canoe. Finally, guided by the Bella Coola, Mackenzie and his crew reached the Pacific Ocean. The inscription ("Alexander Mackenzie from Canada by land 22nd July 1793") he affixed to a rock, using a mixture of vermilion paint and grease, has since been carved into a rock that can be viewed near the town of Bella Coola.

■ *Sir Alexander Mackenzie was the first European to reach both the Pacific and Arctic Oceans by land.*

■ Up the "River of Disappointment"

In June 1789 Mackenzie formed a small crew of five explorers (two of whom brought their wives) and a party of natives led by "English Chief." They set out from Lake Athabasca in four canoes and braved miles of rapids between it and Great Slave Lake. When they reached Great Slave, they found it mostly frozen. The crew made it across the lake with great difficulty and at the loss of one canoe. The entry to the Big River (now called the Mackenzie River) was hidden among dead-end marshes and mud bars but the expedition found it and paddled up the river. Because it initially turned west, Mackenzie believed he had found an important new passage to the Pacific. The river eventually turned north, however, and Mackenzie realized it would not lead to his intended destination. The group ultimately arrived at the Beaufort Sea in the Arctic Ocean and returned home after a 102-day journey. Mackenzie called the river that would eventually bear his name "the River of Disappointment."

The great explorations that Mackenzie, and others such as Simon Fraser and David Thompson, conducted for the North West Company set the stage for the next great conflict in the region. This time the conflict was not between the British and Spanish but rather between the rival fur trading companies, North West and Hudson's Bay.

Hudson's Bay Company

In the late 1660s a group of London merchants funded an exploration to the Hudson Bay region. The promise of a profitable fur trade in the area led Charles II of England to grant the merchants a charter in 1670 that founded the Hudson's Bay Company. The king's charter gave the Hudson's Bay Company a trading monopoly over all the land that was drained by rivers that flowed into the Hudson Bay—a much larger area than was known at the time. The company was charged not only with trading

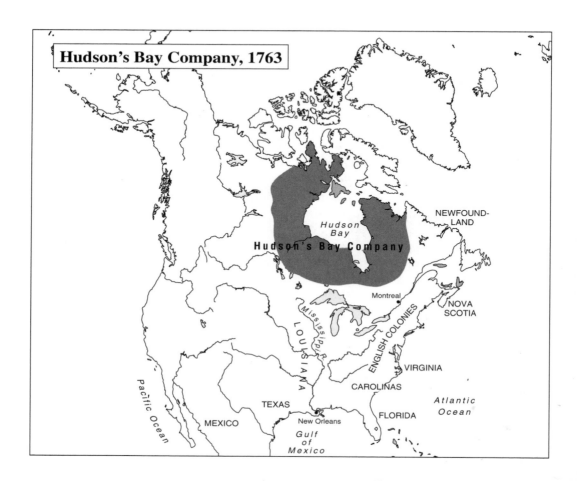

Hudson's Bay Company, 1763

furs—and thus making money for England—but also searching for a possible "northwest passage" to the Orient. The British hoped to find a water route across the top of the North American continent that would be shorter and quicker than the long trip around South America. (It would be almost two centuries before it was proven that such a passage does exist, although it is a winding, often-frozen route of little practical use.)

During the early part of the eighteenth century, the Hudson's Bay Company established a profitable business in the fur trade in the area of present-day Ontario and Quebec. Competition began to develop, however, with other British traders who chose to ignore the company's chartered monopoly. Conflicts arose, too, with the French, since France claimed some of the same land as did England. Battles erupted as French forces tried to take over Hudson's Bay Company forts.

As a result of the fighting, during much of the early eighteenth century company traders became content to remain in their posts and have natives bring furs to them. Fewer and fewer Hudson's Bay Company men seemed willing to trap and explore new territory. This lack of initiative opened the way for a rival company, the North West Company. It was formed in the mid-1780s by a group of Montreal merchants and British fur traders. Under the leadership of bold and adventurous men like Mackenzie and Thompson, the North West Company soon threatened to surpass its stodgy competitor.

The Rival Northwesters

Hudson's Bay Company people often looked down upon the tactics of the Northwesters (as the group was commonly nicknamed). The Northwesters waded through mosquito-filled wetlands and camped on glaciers to find new sources of furs. The Hudson's Bay Company men saw themselves as a more respectable group that gained wealth as Old World English lords had, through the labor of others. The Northwesters, they believed, were the lowly men who earned a profit through their own sweat.

Northwesters seemed unconcerned with their image as they focused on exploring new lands in the west and reaping the benefits of the fruitful fur trade in that area. By the beginning of the nineteenth century, the North West Company had routes through the wilderness that stretched west from Labrador to the Arctic and to the Pacific. The company built forts at almost every important river junction in northern and western Canada as well as in present-day Oregon, Washington, Idaho, Montana, North Dakota, Minnesota, and Wisconsin. The company's profitability depended heavily on its

■ Simon Fraser

Simon Fraser, the next great pathfinder and explorer of the Pacific Northwest, was much in the mold of Alexander Mackenzie: Both were North West Company fur traders of Scottish heritage who started their careers in Montreal. Unlike Scotland-born Mackenzie, Simon Fraser was born near Bennington, Vermont, in the momentous year of 1776. His father remained loyal to the British during the American Revolution and after the war the family, like many other Loyalists, fled north to Canada. At sixteen Simon apprenticed to the North West Company in Montreal and, by the time he was twenty-five, had been sent to Athabasca and made partner. Beginning in 1805 Fraser helped extend the company's fur-trading domain in the northern Rockies.

After Fraser set up a number of forts in the area, the North West Company asked him to explore the river that Mackenzie had followed in part during his landmark expedition of 1793. The company wanted a river trade route from the Rockies to the Pacific and believed that this river, which it mistakenly thought to be the present-day Columbia, was it. In May 1808 Fraser set out with a company of twenty-three men to follow and chart it.

The river presented a difficult challenge. It starts near Yellowhead Pass on the west of the continental divide, not far from towering Mount Robson. The Fraser's source is only about 300 miles (480 kilometers) northeast of Vancouver as the crow flies, but the 850-mile (1,370-kilometer) -long

moving farther and farther outward; it was, in a sense, filling the gap left by the stagnant Hudson's Bay Company. Not long after its formation, the North West Company controlled almost 80 percent of the Canadian fur trade—it ruled the west.

The Sleeping Bear Awakens

The North West Company's success forced the Hudson's Bay Company to reexamine its policy of "sitting by the bay." It began to recognize the shortcomings of merely waiting for the native fur traders to come to the company's forts to trade, rather than actively seeking the furs themselves. Yet, the Hudson's Bay Company also began to appreciate an essential piece of the economic puzzle that it possessed and would not relinquish—the Hudson Bay itself.

The Hudson Bay provided the Hudson's Bay Company with ports that had direct access, through the Hudson Strait and Labrador Sea, into the North Atlantic. Ships could transport furs down the coast, to Quebec, Montreal, Boston, or New York, or across the Atlantic to England. Hudson's Bay is also centrally located in the landmass that was to become Canada.

path the river takes to the Strait of Georgia is anything but direct. It flows first almost due north through the Rocky Mountain Trench before making a U-turn (near present-day Prince George) and heading south and then west toward the Pacific. At various points the river plunges into canyons, some of whose walls rise thousands of feet. Fraser's team took more than a month to navigate 520 miles (840 kilometers) of the demanding river before finally arriving at the mouth near present-day Vancouver. It wasn't until a few years later that the river was named after Fraser by the North West Company explorer David Thompson.

Fraser left the North West Company in 1818 and moved back to Cornwall in present-day Ontario. He bought land, married, fathered nine children, and even took up arms in his early sixties to help defend Canada. In 1862, he and his wife of forty-two years died within a day of each other.

The river and valley that bear his name remain of paramount importance to the province. The Fraser has been hailed as the greatest salmon river in the world. The delta where the Fraser River enters the Strait of Georgia near Vancouver holds the largest population center in western Canada, as well as prime agricultural land. The river valley also provides a channel for segments of the transcontinental highway and railway as they traverse British Columbia. Fraser's name also lives on at the Simon Fraser University in Burnaby, one of the top universities of British Columbia.

The North West Company, unable to establish itself on the Hudson Bay, had to transport their goods tremendous distances. As the Northwesters were branching farther west, their return line for the furs was almost 3,000 miles (4,800 kilometers) overland from the Pacific Northwest just to reach Montreal. At times, up to thirty months would pass before the furs reached their intended destination (where, most likely, they had already been traded for goods long before their arrival).

The rivalry between the two companies ended in 1821 when the Hudson's Bay Company absorbed the North West Company, merging their separate landholdings and forming a truly transcontinental monopoly. The spirit of exploration that Northwesters brought into the combined company endured. As writer Dorthea Calverley has noted about the Northwesters:

> Their individualism, initiative, and free spirit had become a part of the Canadian character, especially in the Western provinces. . . . There is a difference in Western people, a legacy from people like Alexander Mackenzie—a legacy from the old Nor'westers. It is a legacy of overcoming all obstacles, of endurance and courage, of independence and individualism. Westerners are enterprising and non-conformist. We too, are Northwesters in many ways.[7]

Over the next few decades the Hudson's Bay Company controlled the region's trade. But its power was also much more far-reaching, affecting settlement, law enforcement, interactions with native peoples, and more. With the power of the British Crown behind it, and little other established rule in the area, western Canada was held firmly in the grasp of the Hudson's Bay Company.

First Nations in Decline

The merger of 1821 and the gradual influx of settlers created unforeseen tragedy for the native tribes. In the past, the fur traders had essentially viewed the Indians as business partners—it was the Indians who caught the salmon and hunted and trapped the animals that the company needed. The company recognized the useful role the Indians played and nurtured their trust and friendship. Many First Nations people became quite prosperous from trading with the company. When the Hudson's Bay Company gained control over all the land and the added manpower of the North West Company, they needed less help from the Indians.

The coming of settlers led to a decline of wealth and power for the First Nations in an additional way. Many fur traders had versed themselves in the tribal cultures and could recognize the differences between individual tribes. This was not out of idle interest but because the knowledge helped fur

■ *The Hudson's Bay Company establishment on Vancouver Island.*

traders become better and more profitable at their trade. Knowing a tribe's system of rank and leadership pointed the fur traders to the right people in the tribe to conduct business. Settlers, on the other hand, often did not educate themselves about the native culture simply because, for them, there was little to be gained from interaction. Because the Indians did not contribute to the settlers' prosperity, they were viewed as nuisances and obstacles to white expansion.

■ A scene at a Hudson's Bay Company store, where the natives were treated as valued business partners in the early years.

Other factors also caused a decline in native culture:

> The [Hudson's Bay Company] generally treated the native fairly, and their communities thrived. However, the commerce caused the indigenous people to abandon their traditional homesites in favour of settlements closer to the forts for improved trading and protection. The settlers introduced muskets, alcohol, and smallpox, all of which had a devastating effect on the native people. Christian missionaries arrived and set about banning the natives' traditional potlatches and suppressing their languages and culture. Colonization and land ownership conflicts soon followed, and continue to this day.[8]

The Hudson's Bay Company, at least initially, didn't much support the idea of European settlement in the Pacific Northwest. It wanted to use whatever accessible land it could to develop the fur trade, and tried to discourage any settlements it thought might infringe on its land. The monopoly and strict rules of the Hudson's Bay Company angered the settlers that did inevitably come, both east from Canada and north from

■ *The native congre-gation of a church in the Queen Charlotte Islands in 1881.*

the United States. Clearly, even with reduced competition after the merger, the Hudson's Bay Company faced new challenges to its authority.

A History of Diversity and Conflict

The First Nations, the European explorers, and the Hudson's Bay Company each helped define the area of British Columbia, whether through shaping the culture of the land or exploiting its resources for profit. The First Nations were the first settlers of the region, living off the land and discovering its uses and limits. Today, more than ninety thousand people in British Columbia identify themselves as part of the First Nations. Many more who perhaps do not identify themselves as Native Canadian might qualify due to mixed ancestry. (In Canada as a whole, there are as many as 1 million people of aboriginal origin.) First Nations' numbers and influence have fallen since the arrival of the Europeans, but native groups proudly continue the struggle to maintain their unique identities.

The Europeans brought new economic industries as well as more and more people to settle in the area. With the aid of the early business monopolies, they expanded the market for the region's natural resources, including fur, fish, and lumber, from a local one to an international one. This was to have dramatic effects on virtually all aspects of both the society and the land.

Golden
Opportunities

I n the early 1800s, the Pacific Northwest was a remote yet increasingly contested area. Merchants and traders from various countries sailed to the coasts and challenged the Hudson's Bay Company's commercial monopoly. To the south, the United States was growing in power and influence. First Nations people benefited from the trade but also became apprehensive about the gradual loss of control over their lives and lands. Out of this confusion British Columbia would eventually emerge, but only after peoples' burning desire for land and money—and especially gold—helped determine the related issues of boundaries and unity.

And Then There Were Two

Among the four countries that still vied for influence in the Pacific Northwest, two—Russia and Spain—were on the verge of dropping out. The Russians had been trading sea otter furs from the Bering Strait to present-day northern California since the 1780s, at one time claiming a monopoly (routinely ignored by the British and others) all the way down to the 51st parallel. In 1812 the Russians even founded a settlement in northern California. But Russia couldn't sustain its interests as turbulent times in Europe started to demand all of its energies. Despite these pressures, Russia did manage to retain its claim to the huge landmass of present-day Alaska.

Spain, likewise, was no longer following up on explorations it had made to the Pacific Northwest in the 1770s and 1780s. By

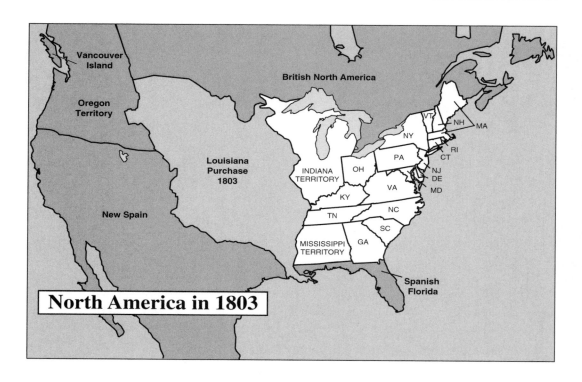

North America in 1803

1800, although it still held huge claims to all the land of the present-day American West Coast, its influence did not extend beyond the 42nd parallel, the present-day boundary between California and Oregon.

This left two major countries, Great Britain and the United States, to compete for power and influence in the land, then largely unexplored by Europeans, of present-day Washington and British Columbia. Great Britain had the early advantage. Its agents, the Hudson's Bay and North West Companies, had explored the area and established relations with the native peoples. Great Britain was still the world's dominant superpower, though the United States had been gaining in power since the War of 1812. As a country with a powerful navy, Great Britain recognized the future potential of a Pacific port.

The United States, on the other hand, had little presence in the early 1800s in the Pacific Northwest, or even in the West in general. The American sea captain Robert Gray may have been the first white to sail into the mouth of the Columbia River back in 1792. (The river was named after his ship, the *Columbia,* and thus eventually supplied the name for the province of British Columbia as well.) Lewis and Clark's famous overland expedition of 1804–1806 to map and explore the area acquired from France in the Louisiana Purchase of 1803 also reached the mouth of the Columbia River. In 1811 the American John Jacob Astor, founder of the Pacific Fur Company, established the first permanent American settlement on the Pacific at Fort Astoria near the mouth of the Columbia. But his venture lasted only two years before British forces destroyed his post during the War of 1812, forcing Astor to sell out to the North West Company. American settlement was then only beginning to trickle west of the Mississippi, and the heavy migrations along the Oregon trail to the West Coast wouldn't begin until the 1840s.

Even though America was overshadowed in the area by the British and the Hudson's Bay Company, the United States was keen to make its presence felt. Merchants and naturalists were sailing to the area, and U.S. presidents from Jefferson onward tried to talk Spain into selling their interests there. So ultimately it was up to the United States and Great Britain to determine how to resolve this minor disagreement: Where exactly on the map did each country's influence begin and end?

The 1818 Compromise

After the War of 1812, American and British diplomats sought to resolve some thorny issues. One of these related to the northern boundary of the Louisiana Territory, the huge wedge of land from the Mississippi to the Rockies that the United States had purchased from France in 1803. The United States and Great Britain addressed a number of these issues in the Convention of 1818, including fishing rights in the Atlantic Ocean (Americans were permitted limited fishing off the coasts of Labrador and Newfoundland) and the northern border of the Louisiana Territory. This line was fixed at the 49th parallel, but only from northern Minnesota to the continental divide on the Rocky Mountains.

In 1818, even after Spain officially renounced its claims to the Pacific Northwest, what to do with the territory was not yet a pressing issue for the United States and Great Britain. The two countries agreed to a joint occupation of the land for ten years (a period that in 1827 would be extended indefinitely) and they agreed to revisit the question of where to draw the boundary from the continental divide west to the Pacific. This delay ultimately led to the loss of a potentially valuable chunk of land—most of present-day Washington State—for Canada and British Columbia, a loss that some Canadians resent to this day.

The Hudson's Bay Company Takes Off

The merger of the Hudson's Bay and North West companies some three years after the Treaty of 1818 helped to increase

British influence over the territory. To keep the Hudson's Bay Company's interests in the colony secure, the company sent a former Northwester, John McLoughlin, to the coastal area. In 1825 McLoughlin set up a post 40 miles (70 kilometers) up the Columbia River (near present-day Portland, Oregon) and called it Fort Vancouver. Fort Vancouver became McLoughlin's headquarters, and from there he controlled much of the fur trade in the area. McLoughlin, said the American lieutenant Neil M. Howison, did "more than any other man toward the rapid development of the resources of the country."[9]

The fur trade flourished, but in subsequent years McLoughlin became increasingly concerned about a growing threat to the south of his fort. Americans had begun to explore the unsettled region to the north of California. At first, only American missionaries began filtering into what was coming to be known as the Oregon Territory. But soon after came the traders and with them the settlers and the merchants, setting up posts, stores, and saloons. As Americans continued to push their way into the territory, conflict over the border seemed inevitable.

In the early 1840s, as more Americans began to drift into the territory, tension mounted. American settlers in the area became increasingly angry at what they called the tyranny of the Hudson's Bay Company, and the settlers took steps to establish their own provincial government. The Hudson's Bay Company determined that it did not have the resources to engage in a head-to-head competition with the United States. So the company decided to retreat and shift its focus to the area north of the Columbia River. McLoughlin asked James Douglas, another Hudson's Bay Company man, to establish a fort on the south end of Vancouver Island. Douglas called his fort Fort Victoria, and it would one day become the capital city of Victoria.

■ *John McLoughlin (top) and James Douglas (bottom), protectors of Hudson's Bay Company interests.*

The Border Dispute Heats Up

The Hudson's Bay Company's territorial worries were not unfounded. When James Polk was running for president of the United States in 1844, one of his main campaign slogans was "54-40 or fight." The slogan referred to a line of latitude that runs more or less through the middle of present-day British Columbia, north of Prince George. (This was the parallel that the Americans and Russians negotiated in 1824, setting the southern boundary for Russia's Alaskan holdings.) Polk's slogan expressed the aggressive new feelings afoot in the United States as it expressed its "manifest destiny" to expand coast to coast. In the years from 1818 to 1844, the United States had grown considerably in military and economic power, having purchased Florida from Spain and separated Texas from Mexico.

By the early 1840s, both the United States and Britain seemed willing to extend the border along the 49th parallel from the Rockies west to the Columbia River. The main dispute centered on the valuable land—much of present-day Washington State—south of the 49th and enclosed by the Columbia River as it wound south and then west to the Pacific.

In addition to the land itself and the Columbia River, both countries wanted control of the Puget Sound. They recognized the deep sound, well protected by the Strait of Juan de Fuca, as a potentially major port. The area where the Columbia River entered the Pacific, on the other hand, had a dangerous bar near its mouth and was thus far inferior as a potential port. California was then a Mexican possession, and in 1835 the Mexicans had declined to sell the port of San Francisco to the Americans for the half-million dollars offered. The United States needed a Pacific port, and the Puget Sound was a good candidate. Great Britain, with a presence already on Vancouver Island, was only slightly less fervid about the sound. They felt, with good reason, that their long-term presence in the area, the fact that they initially explored the area and operated a successful fur-trading business, should give them the right to the land.

Polk's slogan about 54-40 turned out to be bluster. In 1845 the United States became embroiled with Mexico about its land to the west of Texas. The United States won the war that ensued from 1846 to 1848. As a result, Mexico lost about two-fifths of its territory to the growing continental empire of the United States. The timing of the war with Mexico meant, however, that in 1846, as negotiations with Britain on the boundary of the Oregon Territory got underway, Polk was unwilling to risk a second war. Still, American diplomats drove a hard bargain and came away with as much as, and possibly more than, they reasonably could have hoped for: The Oregon Treaty established the 49th parallel as the border between British and U.S. possessions from the Rockies west to the Pacific. The Americans gained the Puget Sound, future site of Seattle and Tacoma, while the British remained in control of Fort Victoria and Vancouver Island.

Even with the treaty verifying British control, Americans continued to migrate into the unsettled territory, and the Hudson's Bay Company officials feared they might lose Vancouver Island or a portion of the mainland. In an effort to hinder further American expansion, the British government

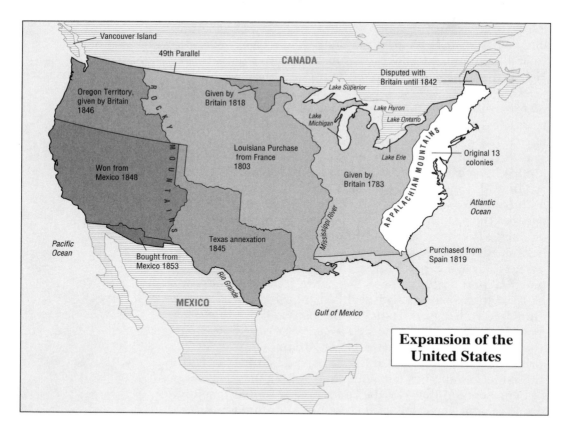

decided Vancouver Island should be settled by Britain to confirm British sovereignty in the area. In 1849, Vancouver Island was established as a Crown colony and handed over to the Hudson's Bay Company to promote settlement and trade.

For a land previously claimed by several countries, a land whose limits were constantly debated, threatened, and pushed, to have an established southern boundary was an important first step in creating an identity for the colony. Another crucial issue related to what type of economy the area could support. The Pacific Northwest was obviously rich in natural resources such as lumber, fish, and minerals. With a port on the Pacific, it was also a natural trade route west to Asia and, if the considerable barriers of distance and geography could be overcome, east to the cities of Toronto, Montreal, and even New York. But in the late 1850s fate threw a wild card—gold—into this mix and put the area's development on fast-forward.

"Gold!"

British Columbia was changed forever in 1858 with the shout of one word, "Gold!" The discovery of gold and the surprising explosion of wealth inevitably introduced immense change, not only to those prospectors who flooded the area but also to the land and to the booming new towns. The native peoples, whose land claims were often pushed aside, and immigrants from China, whose labor was at first welcomed and then resented, were also deeply affected by the Pacific Northwest gold rush.

As the California gold rush was nearing its end, gold-diggers who had not fulfilled their dreams of wealth began traveling north in search of new deposits. They prospected through the Oregon Territory with only minor success, but when they reached the Fraser River Valley in 1858, they found the gold they had been looking for. It did not take long for the news to spread.

Within months of the first discoveries, thousands of prospectors, laborers, outfitters, and assorted footloose characters flooded across the 49th parallel from the south. In addition to the people came an explosion of industry and economy as enterprising business owners thought of ways to profit from the miners. Towns were quickly established. Saloons, hotels, restaurants, and dance halls all opened their doors to capitalize on the miners' new wealth. These towns were appropriately called boomtowns because they were built seemingly overnight from the sudden influx of people and money.

All this prosperity and increase in population did not go unnoticed by England, which again became concerned about

■ *British Columbian miners and merchants stand near their supplies and stores during the gold rush.*

■ Back to the Past in Barkerville

A veteran of California's 1849 gold rush, Welshman Billy Barker was one of many fortune seekers who followed the allure of the nugget to the wilds of the Pacific Northwest in the late 1850s. Billy was no flash-in-the-pan prospector but rather an organizer who thought big. He formed a company and started sinking deep shafts in an area of the Cariboo that others thought unpromising. Finally, in 1862, when his third shaft had reached a depth of more than 50 feet, he hit serious gold.

Barker's strike and the renewal of the gold fever first felt in 1858 created an almost instant town, soon named Barkerville. By the mid-1860s Barkerville claimed to be (and may have been) the biggest city west of Chicago and north of San Francisco. "Individuality characterized the town: small gold claims and lone prospectors seeking permits, private outfitters selling supplies to the prospectors, and entrepreneurs building the town almost overnight," notes the British Columbia Heritage Trust. The town also attracted throngs of Chinese laborers, who came north from California as well as directly from their homeland. Chinese made up perhaps one-quarter of the town's peak population of ten thousand residents.

The unplanned town grew haphazardly into a jumble of uneven board-walks and closely spaced wooden buildings. The buildings faced each other across a narrow main street that followed the sweeping curve of a former creekbed (which had been diverted for panning). Among other things the town was one big fire hazard and in 1868 it did indeed burn to the ground. Gold money was still plentiful enough, however, for prospectors, saloon-keepers, and outfitters to rebuild their cabins, stores, hotels, and churches.

By the late 1870s the gold had begun to become scarce and Barkerville started a slow slide to obscurity. In the 1950s, however, a renewed interest in British Columbia's heritage led the provincial government to start

American influence over the region. In 1858 British authorities established the new mainland colony of British Columbia and appointed the Hudson's Bay Company veteran James Douglas as governor. The rapidly growing new city on the mainland, New Westminster, became the first capital. Vancouver Island remained a separate colony.

The Mainland and Vancouver Combine

Many of the new gold-rush towns were located in remote mountainous areas. In 1862, Governor Douglas, in an attempt to open the southern interior, arranged for the construction of a new 400-mile (650-kilometer) road from the Fraser River Valley to Barkerville in the Cariboo Mountains. Building the road was not an easy task; it took three years and bankrupted the colony in the process.

an ambitious rebuilding and preservation project. The province created the Barkerville Historic Town and sought to bring the town back to its 1860s glory days. It's now one of the most authentic nineteenth-century western towns, as well the site of the oldest surviving Chinatown in North America.

Barkerville is open to the public year-round. No one lives in Barkerville anymore—the last resident died in 1979 and provincial officials say that people represent too much of a fire hazard. During the winter, when few visitors come, Barkerville feels like a true ghost town. But from May to September, when the province offers interpretation and visitor services, the town surges with enthusiastic visitors. An estimated eighty thousand people come annually to pan for gold, ride on a stagecoach, and tour the many authentic buildings. Kids especially get a thrill from the mining demonstrations and street theater performed by costumed actors.

■ *Visitors observe actors in nineteenth-century costume in the historic gold rush town of Barkerville.*

In the mid-1860s, with the gold rush tapering off, thousands of new residents suddenly unemployed, and the new mainland colony deeply in debt, Britain's colonies in the area faced an uncertain future. In 1866, Britain merged Vancouver Island and the mainland into one colony, British Columbia, for greater economic strength. New Westminster gave way to Victoria as the sole capital of the united colony. Only a year later, the people of British Columbia would begin to consider another momentous change: whether to join in a confederation to make the independent country of Canada.

Canada Makes a Land Deal

By the early 1860s it was clear that the colonies no longer wanted to be under British rule, nor was Britain that keen on continuing to shoulder the burden of the colonies' defense. In

■ Vancouver's Gastown

In 1867 a retired riverboat captain named Jack Deighton came to the remote inlet area of the Strait of Georgia's English Bay to set up a tavern. Deighton always had a story to tell or an opinion to voice. His patrons soon dubbed him "Gassy Jack" because of all the hot air he could generate. Sailors and gold miners would stop by Gassy Jack's to get provisions and drink whiskey. The saloon was hardly a fine establishment—brawls and stabbings were almost nightly occurrences—but it gradually became surrounded by the ramshackle wooden buildings and docks of "Gastown." Streets with names like Blood Alley and Gaoler's Mews give an idea of the rough-and-tumble atmosphere of the time.

In the years after 1875, when Gassy Jack died, the new city's name was changed first to Granville, after a British colonial secretary, and finally to Vancouver. The oldest section of the city, however, is still referred to as Gastown. In 1886, when the Canadian Pacific Railway reached Vancouver, the city experienced a flood of people and prosperity. In that year alone, five hundred new buildings—restaurants, hotels, saloons, and houses—were constructed (mostly from wood) in only seventy-five days. Later that year, a scrub fire burned out of control. Within an hour much of Gastown and the young city were smoking ruins; twenty people were killed. The citizens slowly rebuilt the city using brick and stone rather than wood. In the years that followed, however, Gastown became a somewhat

September 1864, representatives from Nova Scotia, New Brunswick, Newfoundland, and Prince Edward Island met to discuss the possibility of a maritime union (a union of the Atlantic provinces). Two leading delegates from a coalition of parties representing the Province of Canada (including what would become Ontario and Quebec) wrangled an invitation to the meeting. At the conference, the Province of Canada delegates quickly gained agreement to expand the idea of a maritime union to a federal union—a confederation of provinces united as one nation. Within three years the provincial representatives had a confederation agreement to present to London. In 1867, the British Parliament voted to accept the British North American Act, basically allowing the provinces to vote for inclusion in a Canadian confederation or for continuation as colonies of the crown. On July 1, 1867, the provinces of Ontario, Quebec, Nova Scotia, and New Brunswick united to form the Dominion of Canada. (Prince Edward Island and Newfoundland had second thoughts; they joined later, in 1873 and 1949, respectively.)

One of the first orders of business for the new confederation was to secure title to the vast landholdings of the Hud-

neglected area as development concentrated to its south and west.

By the 1960s, Gastown was so down-and-out that it was in danger of being razed for development. But the local community rallied support for a renewal of the area, and in 1971 the government declared Gastown a historic area and saved it from destruction. Currently, the Gastown section of Vancouver is a quaint shopping district with cobblestone streets, antique street lamps, and tree-lined paths. The streets contain galleries, souvenir shops, furniture stores, restaurants, pubs, and bars. Visitors can see the famous Gastown steam-powered clock, designed in 1875 though not built until a century later. A tune rings through its pipes every fifteen minutes. On the corner of Carrall and Water Streets, approximately where Gassy Jack's saloon once stood, Gastown's visitors can also see a statue of the city's colorful founder, poised atop a whiskey barrel.

■ *The famous statue of Jack Deighton, or Gassy Jack, in the Gastown section of Vancouver.*

son's Bay Company. The charter granted the company by King Charles II almost two centuries earlier still made it the legal possessor of the huge tract of virtually unpopulated land called "Rupert's Land." Rupert's Land covered an area many times the size of the newly formed Canada, extending hundreds of miles in all directions from the shores of Hudson Bay. Rupert's Land acted as a physical barrier that separated British Columbia from the newly formed Canada.

Canada was afraid that, if it didn't act quickly, British Columbia would become more closely allied with the United States and possibly even consider statehood. Already, a significant part of British Columbia's population consisted of American gold seekers, traders, and merchants. Many of British Columbia's businesses had created strong commercial ties to the new states of California and Oregon. Trade and commerce were also linked to the United States after the first transcontinental railway was completed there in 1869. British Columbia could now ship goods to the East Coast by sailing them south to San Francisco and then loading them on the rails for the journey east, rather than having to rely on the arduous overland journey by wagon or the lengthy sail around the tip of South America.

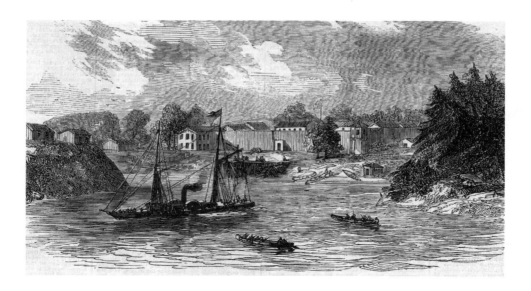

■ *Victoria in 1866 after being named capital of the colony of British Columbia.*

British Columbia's common bonds to the Americans did not go unnoticed by the new provinces of Canada. Realizing that losing British Columbia to the United States would mean Canada would have no access to the Pacific, Canada quickly took steps to bring British Columbia into the confederation. In 1869 the new nation bought Rupert's Land from the Hudson's Bay Company for $1.5 million. This removed an obvious roadblock to enticing British Columbia into the confederation, but another remained: Even after selling its huge Rupert's stake, the Hudson's Bay Company still had a powerful hold in British Columbia through the fur trade, and it was in no rush to see British Columbia join the Confederation of Canada.

Overcoming Company Opposition

The Hudson's Bay Company liked things as they were. It wanted British Columbia to remain a Crown colony so that the company could retain its dominant hold on the economy. The company feared it would lose its control over the region and its lucrative fur trade if the colony were to become a province. Moreover, the company was joined in its opposition to confederation by many of the local merchants. They preferred becoming part of the United States, since this would more quickly open up trade routes and bring new business into the area.

The British government, on the other hand, preferred a Canadian British Columbia to an American British Columbia. Britain wanted to lessen its presence in the Pacific region,

■ Amor de Cosmos

The man who was to become one of the most influential journalists in British Columbia history, as well also its second premier, was born William Alexander Smith in Nova Scotia in 1825. A wanderer as a young man who followed the gold rush to California, in 1854 Smith legally changed his name to Amor de Cosmos (lover of the world), a name he constructed from a mixture of French and Greek. "He was a curious mixture of vanity and intellectual capability," said James Robert Anderson in his *Notes and Comments on Early Days and Events in British Columbia, Washington, and Oregon.*

■ *Journalist, politician, and second premier of British Columbia Amor de Cosmos.*

In 1858 de Cosmos moved to Victoria as the gold rush was erupting in the Fraser River valley. He quickly started a newspaper, the *British Colonist*, and began to use it as a sounding board for his ideas on the need for responsible government, free schooling, and unity between the island and mainland communities. Elected to the Vancouver Island colonial assembly in 1863, he soon became an outspoken opponent of Governor Douglas's administration. De Cosmos accused Douglas of favoring the Hudson's Bay Company in his administrative decisions because of Douglas's connections to the company.

In 1867 de Cosmos was elected to the British Columbia legislature and to the Parliament in Ottawa. He became a staunch supporter of British Columbia joining the confederation. Not content to work only through the legislature, he formed the pro-union Confederation League and organized grassroots support. His efforts were instrumental in the province's successful admission to the confederation in 1871.

In 1872 de Cosmos won the vote to become the province's second premier (and its first Canadian-born premier), a position he held until 1874. He remained a member of Parliament until 1882 and died in 1897. He's now well remembered as a forward-thinking, if sometimes eccentric, man of great intelligence who played a prominent role in steering British Columbia into the twentieth century.

but as a check on American power Great Britain did not want the United States to acquire British Columbia. Therefore, the British government appointed Anthony Musgrove, a former governor of Newfoundland, as the new governor of British Columbia and advised him to push British Columbia to join the confederation. The British suggested that a good way to convince the people of British Columbia to join would be to support the proconfederation movement led by local businessman John Robson and newspaperman Amor de Cosmos. Musgrove and these two men did indeed turn out to be key figures.

British Columbia Becomes a Province

Governor Musgrove immediately appointed a committee to negotiate a union with Canada. Robson, leader of a party called the "Mainland Reformists," also agreed with the idea of the confederation, and along with de Cosmos supported a motion in British Columbia's legislature asking for entry. Several times the motion was brought before the legislature, but legislators backed by the Hudson's Bay Company continued to outvote it. De Cosmos, disheartened by the legislature's actions, in 1868 formed the Confederation League, the first political party in British Columbia. In 1869, the league held a conference at Yale on the Fraser River to discuss conditions under which British Columbia might agree to join the confederation.

Realizing what an important role it would play in the new nation as the sole outlet to the Pacific, British Columbia refused to join the confederation unless Canada would meet certain conditions. British Columbia insisted that Canada pay the large debt the colony had left over after the end of the gold rush. British Columbia also insisted that Canada undertake a public works program that would build roads to link the isolated colony to the rest of Canada. Canada not only agreed to British Columbia's terms, but also committed to building a railroad that would link British Columbia to the rest of Canada within ten years.

In 1870, after an election led to a legislature more favorable to confederation, the Confederation League sent three delegates to Ottawa to negotiate with members of the confederation. With all the terms agreed to, British Columbia became Canada's sixth province on July 20, 1871 (Manitoba had joined the original four in 1870), and soon held its first provincial election, electing John Foster McCreight as its first premier.

Linking British Columbia to the East

The Confederation did not fall short of its promises, and the railroad eventually did come to British Columbia. Andrew Onderdonk, an American engineer, was contracted to construct the section of the railroad line that began at the Pacific

■ The Building of the Canadian Pacific Railway

Railroad construction in British Columbia in the late nineteenth century was backbreaking and dangerous work. Tunnels needed to be dynamited through mountains, railbeds carved from rocky slopes, steep canyons forded by wooden bridges. Progress was costly, in money and manpower—two workers died for every mile the Canadian Pacific Railway advanced. It wasn't a job for everyone, but one group in particular willingly took on the work: immigrants from China.

These were mostly young, single men who, prompted by overcrowding, food shortages, and lack of opportunity in China, left their families to seek a decent wage in the Pacific Northwest. As followers of the philosophy of Confucianism, which taught acceptance of life's hardships, they were the types of diligent, uncomplaining workers needed for jobs like mining and railway building. Between 1880 and 1885, the Canadian Pacific Railway hired some seventeen thousand Chinese, not only as laborers but as cooks, gardeners, and carpenters. Most sent much of their earnings back to their families in China.

An estimated one thousand Chinese returned home after the transcontinental railway was completed in 1885. The bulk of the Chinese, however, stayed on in the New World and established restaurants, laundries, and other businesses. One noted success story, Yip Sang, went on to become the Chinese agent for the Canadian Pacific Railway and then a successful landowner and businessman in Vancouver. Unfortunately, during the early 1900s an anti-Chinese backlash developed among many whites. British Columbia prohibited the Chinese from voting, and the national government started to demand an expensive "head tax" from any Chinese wanting to immigrate into the country. In 1907 Vancouver suffered a nasty anti-Chinese riot that spilled into the city's Chinatown, followed by a three-day strike on the part of Chinese workers that crippled the city.

For many years, Chinese Canadians were subject to harassment and prejudice. Around the time of World War II, when China was seen as a brave ally to the Allied forces, public opinion softened. Today, almost eighty thousand Chinese Canadians live in Vancouver's Chinatown district, which is the third largest in the world behind San Francisco's and New York's. Visitors come to see the many stores, eat in the restaurants, and visit traditional acupuncturists or Chinese healers. In recent years British Columbia has taken steps to recognize and commemorate the role of Chinese workers in its early history.

coast and moved inland, where it was to link up with the line approaching from the east. Among other tasks, fifteen tunnels had to be built along the route and massive expanses of bridgework had to be constructed across valleys. The huge scope of

■ *Workers lay track on the Canadian Pacific Railway in British Columbia. The railroad was completed in 1885.*

the project caused Onderdonk to quickly run out of workers, so he began importing them from China. It took five years, but on November 7, 1885, the railway to the Pacific was completed, and Donald A. Smith, one of the railroad's financiers, drove in the last spike at Craigellachie in Eagle Pass, B.C.

As Eric Lucas, author of *Hidden British Columbia*, has noted,

On June 13, 1887, a Pacific clipper ship, the SS *Abyssinia,* sailed past Siwash Rock, beneath two peaks called The Lions, through the tide-scoured First Narrows and into the jade waters of [Vancouver's] Burrard Inlet. It offloaded bales of Chinese tea and silk, most of which were quickly shifted to a rail car to begin the lengthy journey through the Canadian Rockies, across the prairies and on to London. Vancouver's international commercial tale had begun.[10]

The search for a northwest passage that had inspired the founding of the Hudson's Bay Company more than two centuries earlier had proven unrealistic, but trains could cross the continent even faster than ships could sail the same distance. The railway produced so much business that eventually it could not meet the demand. Two new lines, the Grand Trunk Pacific and the Canadian Northern, were added in 1914 and 1915, respectively. British Columbia was at last linked to the rest of Canada, and to the world.

The rate of growth and progress sped up in British Columbia. The fishing and logging industries began to flourish. The first pulp and paper mill opened on Powell River in 1912 and sawmills were built on Vancouver Island. Mining camps sprouted in the interior, and oil and natural gas were discovered in the northeast. Industry thrived, the population increased, and many companies used the natural resources around them to carve out business opportunities. British Columbia's modern economy and identity had been successfully set in motion by the driving forces of the boundary resolution, the gold rush, the confederation, and the need for better trade routes.

Life in British Columbia Today

B ritish Columbia in the twenty-first century is a diverse and modern society, yet a significant percentage of its residents are employed by traditional occupations such as logging and fishing, the resource-dependent industries that helped establish the province two centuries ago. These jobs still require a commitment to hard work, and a willingness to face uncomfortable and sometimes hazardous conditions, but new technologies have transformed the work in important ways. Increasingly, the people of British Columbia also work in manufacturing, high-tech, ecotourism, and other new industries.

Daily life for many of the urban and suburban people of the province is not that much different from the experience of other Canadians, though the many outstanding recreational options open to British Columbians have gained them a reputation as an easy-going and fun-loving crowd. "This is the only province of the ten," according to one columnist, "that is dedicated to hedonism."[11] Pleasure seeking comes in many forms, of course, and many citizens of British Columbia gain much of their pleasure from taking advantage of the high-quality educational, health care, and social opportunities the province affords.

The Outdoor Economy

With some 64 percent of British Columbia being covered by forests and the demand for wood and paper as strong as ever,

■ *Two loggers attach drag lines to felled lumber. Logging is one of the province's main industries.*

logging remains important to British Columbia's economy. Although the industry now directly employs only about 5 percent of the overall provincial population, in some areas it can account for the livelihood of almost an entire community. Increasingly, however, loggers must be willing to relocate to areas where trees can be legally cut. Often these men and women leave their homes and families for months at a time to live in logging camps near the site in which they are working. The logging camps are usually in remote areas where there are few roads, bare-bones housing, and little company other than fellow loggers. In the past, logging in these areas was a risky undertaking: If an accident or emergency occurred, medical help was often hours away. Today, with improved equipment and better communications, the profession is somewhat safer. Loggers, however, are still faced with problems relating to equipment failure, harsh weather conditions, and even being attacked verbally—and occasionally physically—by environmental protesters. Because of their jobs, loggers are often blamed for the decisions made by their employers.

Other resources that British Columbia possesses in almost as much abundance as trees are rivers and coastal waters. The huge numbers of fish that swim in these waters support a multibillion-dollar provincial industry. In fact, British Columbia leads all the Canadian provinces in fishing revenue, surpassing even the Atlantic provinces. Tens of thousands of residents are involved in commercial fishing, including increasing numbers working for fish processors, aquaculture operations such as salmon farming, and sport fishing enterprises. The mighty salmon supports much of this diverse industry but the province is also rich in other types of fish such as cod, herring, and trout. Throughout the province, every day of the year sees men and women rising in the early morning hours to use rods, nets, and traps in pursuit of their daily catch. The high cost of the tools needed for commercial success, ranging from a boat to high-tech radar scanners, has led to the commercial fishing industry being increasingly dominated by large companies. Regulations and restrictions necessary to protect fish stocks from decline have also affected small-scale independent fishermen. The challenges and uncertainties of the fishing life have led fewer young people to choose fishing as a career compared to previous years. Rather, this younger generation is choosing to move to the large cities to pursue other opportunities.

Of the traditional ways of earning a living in British Columbia, perhaps the one that has changed the least is farming. Although high-tech machinery and the advent of super-sized farms have radically altered the way farmers grow wheat on the expansive plains of Alberta, for example, the challenges of geography and climate have caused farming in British Columbia to remain mostly small scale and diversified. The most fertile area is the low-lying southern river valleys, which offer the province's longest growing season and most temperate climate. Farms in the Fraser River valley and southwestern

■ *A seiner boat fishing for sockeye salmon spreads its net off Vancouver Island.*

■ Farming on Water

The fastest growing part of British Columbia's fishing industry is aquaculture—raising fish on a "water farm." The province today has approximately eighty active aquaculture farms, most growing salmon but also shellfish, trout, and scallops. Farm-raised salmon now account for one-third of British Columbia's salmon industry, making the province the fourth-largest producer of farmed salmon in the world (after Norway, Chile, and the United Kingdom). Most of B.C.'s salmon farms are on the northeast coast of Vancouver Island and in rural mainland sounds. These farms now employ some twenty-five hundred workers and generate an annual product value of almost $300 million.

As with a land farm, salmon farms start from seed. In this case, the seeds are salmon eggs, typically from Atlantic salmon or chinook. (Atlantic salmon have been found to grow faster than the native Pacific species; one serious drawback to Atlantic salmon, however, is that if they escape into the wild they could compete with and possibly take over the habitat of these native species.) Salmon eggs are raised in onshore hatcheries. Upon hatching the baby smolts spend a few months in freshwater rearing tanks before being moved to the offshore saltwater farms, preferably located where there is cool water and regular tides (to flush away wastes such as uneaten feed and fish feces).

The salmon farms come in various sizes and shapes but most are a series of large, netted, metal-framed cages suspended in the water from floating pontoons. Long walkways surround the pontoons to allow employees to feed and care for the fish. A walkway may also connect to the shore or to a "floating house" where fish feed is kept and employees eat and sleep. Other salmon farms can be reached only by boat.

Working on a salmon farm requires a combination of skills ranging from computer use to the hard physical labor of lugging around heavy bags of feed. Much of the work revolves around making sure the fish are being

coastal regions produce dairy (accounting for 90 percent of all the milk in the province) and poultry products as well as fruit and produce. The Okanagan and Kootenay regions specialize in tree fruits (apples, apricots, peaches), berries and wine grapes, and garden vegetables. The central interior of British Columbia is cattle raising country, and the Peace River valley is known for its grain production.

Life in the Cities

While logging, fishing, and other resource-dependent jobs are still vital parts of British Columbia's economy, even more of the province's citizens are employed in the cities in industries ranging from software development to pharmaceuticals. As is

fed properly, watching for any diseases that may develop, and checking the equipment—the marine environment means lots of upkeep on nets, cages, and pontoons. The day-to-day concerns can be daunting, including the environmental impact of waste on water quality and seabed life; escape prevention; and the effects of feed-added drugs and pesticides on fish health. The most successful salmon farmers need a background not only in marine ecology but business, public relations, and regulation compliance.

■ *A fish farmworker nets salmon from a pen during the harvest.*

the case in other parts of Canada as well, the young people of British Columbia are increasingly gravitating to the cities and the jobs available in them. Vancouver and Victoria are the province's largest and best-known cities, but there are many others, including Prince Rupert, Prince George, Kamloops, and Dawson Creek, known for being thriving and livable.

Vancouver is the largest city in British Columbia and the third largest in all of Canada. The city is built on a peninsula with the Burrard Inlet to the north and the delta of the Fraser River to the south. This area provides a magnificent setting for the city, as the compact skyline is backed by the snow-capped Coast Mountains. As the travel writer Jan Morris has noted, "Vancouver enjoys one of the most splendid of all city settings—better than San Francisco's, because of the greenness,

■ *The thriving city of Vancouver boasts a multicultural population, including a large Chinese community.*

better than Sydney's, because of the mountains all around, rivaled perhaps only by Rio and Hong Kong. It is almost as though the surroundings have been artificially landscaped, on the most colossal scale, and this necessarily gives the city an exhibition flavour, as if consciously on display."[12]

Vancouver's future was assured when the Canadian Pacific Railroad selected the Burrard Inlet area as the western terminus of its transcontinental railway. Today, the city of Vancouver is home to slightly more than half a million people with over a million more living in its suburbs. Vancouver's population is a multicultural mix of Italian, Greek, German, Indian, Vietnamese, and Chinese. In fact, Vancouver contains one of the largest Chinese populations in North America. Vancouver is also home to the University of British Columbia and the Vancouver and Maritime museums.

A Diverse Society

The social culture of British Columbia has changed dramatically from the European-dominated nineteenth century. Today more than one-third of the residents of Vancouver are members of a "visible minority," meaning non-Caucasian in race or color. British Columbia is a culturally diverse province with African Canadians, Asian Canadians, and the native First Nations groups all playing vital roles in the growth and development of the province. British Columbia, in concert with Canada as a whole, has taken steps to encourage people of all races to take active positions in society.

■ British Columbia's Quaint Capital City

Victoria, with a population of only seventy-five thousand, is a small city but its enviable location, role as provincial capital, and pristine condition allow it to play a central role in British Columbia life. Victoria is widely known for, and extremely proud of, its British heritage. As tourists wander through the streets, they are welcomed by colorful English gardens, grand British architecture, a replica of the cottage of Anne Hathaway (Shakespeare's wife), and exquisite shops and cafés on cobblestone streets. Visitors can have afternoon tea and crumpets at the Empress Hotel and take a red double-deck bus like those found in London. Victoria is commonly called "The City of Gardens" and "The Best Bloomin' City" because its weather conditions are ideal for flowering plants and trees to maintain a long blossom period. Visitors to Victoria are often greeted in the spring with baskets overflowing with flowers hanging from the old English lampposts.

Victoria is located on the southern end of Vancouver Island and has a mild, Mediterranean-like climate with moderate rainfall and lots of sunshine. Because of the pleasing climate and Old World charm, Victoria has become a destination for many retirees. In fact, 21 percent of Victoria's population is over sixty-five. Due in part to its climate and scenic beauties, the city has maintained a comfortable and economically prosperous way of life—so comfortable in fact that in a Canadian survey, Victoria residents reported a higher level of satisfaction with their city than did the residents of any other city.

■ *Flowers and old-fashioned lampposts lend charm to the parliament building in Victoria.*

Although British Columbia is a multicultural province, many individuals choose to live in closely knit single-heritage communities. Vancouver's Chinatown is one example. Whereas in the past, such a choice may have been made for greater

■ *Vancouver's China-town helps to preserve the traditions of Chinese Canadians.*

physical security, today it also reflects a willingness to help preserve cultural traditions.

Many First Nations groups in British Columbia are actively seeking ways to rejuvenate their culture and prevent the dispersal of their young into the cities. Even though Indians do not have to pay federal or provincial income taxes as long as they live and work on the Indian reserve, many of the younger generation Indians feel that the opportunities in the cities outweigh these tax benefits. As of 1996, only 44 percent of British Columbia's total native population of ninety-four thousand lived on reservations.

Despite the departure of their young to the metropolitan areas, and the many difficulties the First Nations groups still endure, for the most part their future is promising. Since the 1960s, there have been gradual improvements in the conditions of First Nations' housing, education, and health. In 1990, it was estimated that over 65 percent of Indians twenty-five years of age had had at least twelve years of education. The current health record of Indians is also improving as living standards on the reservations are raised. Today, alcoholism remains the most serious health care issue for Native Canadians, with the related conditions of chronic liver disease and cirrhosis of the liver the two leading causes of death.

A Progressive Educational System

British Columbia's economic and cultural diversity has inspired the province to develop an educational system that is flexible enough to meet the needs of its students. The Public School Act of 1872 established the basis of the school system in British Columbia, stating that education would be free and mandatory for all children ages seven to fifteen. Currently, British Columbia has seventy-five public school districts housing almost two-thousand schools, which are comanaged by the provincial government and local school officials. Funding is established every year by the provincial government

based on the cost of programs, with the funds then being allocated to the districts to manage. Since 1972, schools have had to follow a core curriculum set up by the Ministry for Education for grades K–12. The ministry also provides guidelines that define the specific learning outcomes of the curriculum.

The distinctive glass façade of the University of British Columbia's Museum of Anthropology.

Like British Columbia's K–12 system, the province's universities and other institutes of higher education are widely recognized for their ability to serve a diverse population. The largest and most well known higher education facility in British Columbia is the University of British Columbia, which was established in 1914 and is almost an entire city in itself. The university consists of over five hundred buildings on an extensive campus and offers studies in such fields as engineering, arts, business, forestry, law, and medicine. The university is renowned for its Museum of Anthropology as well as its Botanical Garden, which has ten thousand different trees, shrubs, and flowers planted over seventy acres and also includes the Japanese-inspired Nitobe Memorial Garden.

Simon Fraser University is sometimes referred to as "Vancouver's other university" because its main Burnaby campus (SFU also has a downtown Vancouver campus) is located near the massive University of British Columbia. This is an unfair characterization, however, of a notable institution. Named after the famous British Columbia explorer, Simon Fraser

■ Making Voting Easy

Voting is of such high priority to the people of British Columbia that special voting places are constructed at remote sites, such as logging and mining camps, to allow the opportunity to vote to workers and residents who are eligible but are not able to make it home to their assigned district. In addition to setting up remote polling places, the government also tries to encourage all its citizens to vote by providing translators or hiring electoral officials who are fluent in local languages in areas where English may not be the primary language of residents. Qualified voters (Canadian citizens at least eighteen years old who have resided in British Columbia for at least six months) may also register at the time of voting, as long as they can provide two pieces of personal identification showing their name, current address, and signature. In these ways, British Columbia is striving to make the voices of all its citizens heard in the legislative process both nationally and on the provincial level.

was opened in 1965 and focuses much of its curriculum on science, business administration, education, and architecture. The Canadian magazine *Maclean's* recently ranked SFU second among the nation's comprehensive universities (those with a significant amount of research activity and a wide range of programs at the undergraduate and graduate levels, including professional degrees). Many of its graduates, as well as those of the province's other public university, the University of Victoria, go on to hold prominent positions in British Columbia business and industry.

A Lively Political Scene

British Columbia's provincial government is structured in way that is similar to the federal government. The provincial government is headed by a premier (similar to a president or prime minister) and a cabinet. These positions are filled from the dominant local political party, such as the Liberal, New Democratic, or Social Credit. The premier does not serve a specific term; rather, he or she can be voted out of office whenever another party puts together a stronger coalition. This led to, for example, British Columbia having six premiers in the period 1991 to 2001, with two ruling for less than a year. The provincial legislature consists of one member from each of the seventy-five electoral districts, elected for a term not to exceed five years. Some of these legislative members are chosen for the cabinet to head one of the sixteen administrative departments, such as labor, agriculture, and health care.

Like the other Canadian provinces, British Columbia controls its schools, hospitals, local roads, railroads, local governments, and the administration of justice. British Columbia can tax its residents and visitors to raise funds and administers personal income taxes, sales taxes, taxes on hotel/motel rooms, and other taxes. The province also retains control over its public lands and natural resources. Nationally, British Columbia voters elect thirty-four members of its Parliament to the 301-seat House of Commons in Ottawa. British Columbia is also represented in the Senate by six senators and on the Supreme Court of Canada by at least one judge.

Health Care for One and All

When a resident of British Columbia needs medical attention, he or she can choose a physician, outpatient clinic, or emergency room and use to pay for the services a special health insurance card issued by the province to all eligible residents. Filling out insurance forms, paying deductibles, and making copayments are all unnecessary, much to the relief of patients and health care providers alike. Thus, the people of British Columbia do not have to pay directly for physicians' services.

■ *British Columbia's parliament building in the capital, Victoria.*

This universal health care system, known to residents of British Columbia as Medicare, provides access to universal, comprehensive health care coverage. The federal government sets the principles and standards for the health care system, and it is the duty of the individual provinces to plan, finance, and evaluate their hospitals, physicians, and health care services. This system is not "socialized medicine," in that the government does not directly employ doctors and other health care providers. Rather, doctors are private practitioners who are paid on a fee-for-service basis.

Today, over 95 percent of all hospitals in the province are operated as private, not-for-profit organizations that are primarily accountable to the community they serve, not the provincial administration. This means that the hospitals have

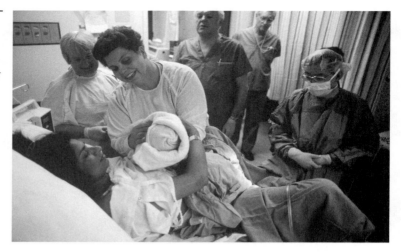

■ *Universal health care allows this Vancouver woman to receive care during childbirth without paying for it directly.*

control over the money they are granted and can tailor it to their communities' needs as long as they stay within the operative budgets set by the provincial administration. The remaining 5 percent of hospitals consist of additional facilities, such as those for long-term care, that are funded primarily by direct patient payments. Other health care professionals, such as dentists, work outside of the health care system unless the patient requires in-hospital treatment. British Columbia is striving to maintain its reputation for top-notch health care and a high ranking worldwide for health-related measurements such as low infant mortality and long average life spans.

A Land of Diverse and Varied Lives

British Columbia's diverse geography is mirrored by its society, which includes everybody from rural loggers to urban dancers. As a popular regional guide recently noted,

> British Columbia is often called the California of Canada, with Canada's most temperate climate, a vibrant film community, a visible and powerful gay and lesbian community, and a soft-focus New Age patina. However, British Columbia is also the Idaho of Canada, the Washington State of Canada, and incidentally, the Asia of Canada. In terms of cultural diversity and competing interests, there's a lot going on here.[13]

Arts and Culture

B ritish Columbia prides itself on being the home of many exceptional artists and performers, a number of whom have gone on to achieve national and even world renown. The province's rich artistic heritage is due in part to cultural diversity—the many ethnic groups, from First Nations to Europeans to Asian Americans, create a lively social scene that is often mined for insights by playwrights, novelists, singers, and others. The exceptional natural setting is also an asset for painters and artists of all types.

Then, too, there is British Columbia's lively reputation as "BeeCee," the most freewheeling and action-packed part of Canada. Undoubtedly, the province's independent and quirky self-image acts as a magnet for creative people, even if it causes somewhat mixed feelings among provincial government officials more interested in attracting conventional businesses. The government of British Columbia, however, wholeheartedly supports arts and culture, proudly showcasing individual creativity by funding film boards, museums, hockey rinks, and more. But, as the province's Cultural Service Branch states, "The arts also promote social cohesion by providing a bridge between the diverse groups who have made their homes in British Columbia."[14]

A Painter's Paradise

Until the early twentieth century, Canadian artists of European descent were typically trained in the styles and techniques of the

■ *A painting of totem poles by British Columbian artist Emily Carr.*

Old World masters. Many talented Canadian painters created distinguished works, but it couldn't be said that a distinctly Canadian style or school developed. Even landscapes often suggested the tame scenery of Europe rather than the uniquely wild panoramas of the New World. This lack of Canadian identity began to change when the famous "Group of Seven" formed in 1920 and put on its first joint exhibit. Rejecting European models, these innovative Canadian painters, from varying backgrounds and locations, created the foundation for a school of painting that would record and reinforce a distinctly Canadian identity.

Among the many Canadian artists who have since followed their lead, British Columbia's eccentric but immensely talented Emily Carr has gained the greatest recognition for her bold paintings of Pacific Northwest totems and landscapes. A contemporary of the men in the Group of Seven, in the 1920s she had already visited First Nations sites and depicted totems and other native cultural objects in her paintings. When Carr had a number of her paintings included alongside works of the Group of Seven in a 1927 exhibition, she was able to experience their distinctly Canadian style and was herself liberated to develop her own personal, though still uniquely Canadian, style. A critique of one of her paintings notes that "Where previously she had sought to provide documentation of the poles and had, to some degree, sublimated her own artistic expression in doing so, she was now trying to convey both her deep respect for these sculptural monuments and her own connection to the forests of British Columbia."[15]

Many of the evocative, highly stylized paintings she created in the 1930s are now considered masterpieces—one of her paintings recently sold for 1 million dollars at auction. The renewed appreciation for Carr is evidenced by the recent "Places of Their Own" exhibit, which was shown in Toronto, Vancouver, and elsewhere. It featured Carr, America's Georgia O'Keeffe, and Mexico's Frida Kahlo as the three pioneering female artists of the twentieth century. Along with a genius for artistic expression they shared a fascination with native culture.

■ Emily "Laughing One" Carr

Emily Carr was born in Victoria in 1871, sharing British Columbia's birth-date as a province of Canada. Her parents died when she was in her teens and she was raised for a few years by an older sister. From early in her life Emily showed an interest in art along with a decidedly independent bent. As a young woman she traveled to study art in San Francisco, London, and Paris, and then taught classes at several art schools in Vancouver.

She struggled to support herself as an artist, once famously declaring, "I don't give a whoop if the public likes my stuff or not—and they don't." She never married and she seemed content to go off for long periods to live and paint among the native cultures. In her best paintings she used vivid greens and blues to evoke the cycles of nature as they merge with the everyday life of the Indian village.

The public was slow to appreciate her talents and in 1913 she had to build and run a lodging house in Victoria to support herself. In 1920, anthropologist Marius Barbeau discovered her early work and helped exhibit a number of her paintings at the National Gallery in Ottawa. After her exposure to the Group of Seven in the 1920s, the more personal and dynamic paintings of the early 1930s gained her an increasing reputation as an artist of national merit.

In the best British tradition, Carr was memorably eccentric. In her later life she was completely enamored of pets. These included unconventional pets like squirrels and rats, some of which she liked to put in a baby carriage and push down the prim and proper streets of Victoria, perhaps with her pet monkey on a leash. Carr was not afraid to buck public opinion on more serious issues, such as the struggles of the native people. A missionary once asked Carr to help convince Indian parents she knew to send their children to an "industrial boarding school," a school which promoted the unlearning of native culture. Carr flatly refused, saying that such schools made children ashamed of their Indian heritage.

Carr used her notoriety to good effect in a number of books she penned in the years before her death in 1945, including *The House of All Sorts* (about her boardinghouse days) and *Klee Wyck*, her prize-winning autobiography. (Klee Wyck means "laughing one," a name given her by the Nootka.) Emily Carr is remembered as a multitalented artist and Canada's premier woman painter. The Vancouver Art Gallery now houses the largest group of her paintings, and her home on Government Street is now a museum. Through the cutting-edge Emily Carr Institute of Art and Design, she's also influenced such modern British Columbia artists as painter Jack Shadbolt, filmmaker Wendy Trilby, and novelist Douglas Coupland (*Generation X*).

■ *The painted wood carvings on totem poles represent ancestors and mythological figures.*

A Rich Tradition of Native Art

The Group of Seven and Emily Carr prompted a generation of British Columbia painters to take inspiration from the province's abundant natural beauty, its wildlife, and its unique cultural heritage. The influence of the Group of Seven and Carr also served to spotlight the creativity and the technical skill evident in the art of the First Nations. The intricately carved and beautifully painted wooden totems are the most famous native works, but artists and artisans of various tribes also created sublime works of jewelry, textile, ceremonial masks, and headdresses. As writer Donald Carroll has noted,

When England's master mariner Captain James Cook landed on the unexplored shores of what is now British Columbia in 1778, he was met by a surprise: an unknown but highly developed Indian culture whose every object, however utilitarian, was made with style and artistry. Living in an abundant but inaccessible region, such tribes as the Haida, Kwakiutl, and Tsimshian were the heirs to a centuries-old tradition of fine craftsmanship which, continued to the present day, has led to their masks, amulets, and other objects being ranked among the world's most prized examples of ethnic art.[16]

Common themes included symbolic use of animals to represent traits of ancestors, or to portray emotions, hopes, and fears. For example, the owl was often a symbol of death, the raven of bravery and cunning, the eagle of peace and friendship, and the killer whale of sadness and mourning.

"Hollywood North"

The thriving visual arts scene in the Pacific Northwest includes not only ancient techniques like totem building but that most modern art of filmmaking. As the third largest (after Los Angeles and New York) film production center in North America, the Vancouver area is becoming known as "Hollywood North." Southern British Columbia has a history of independent filmmaking and film production that goes back to the 1920s. It now boasts a deep pool of talented actors, directors, camera operators, animators, producers, and technicians. The province is home to two major established studios and many smaller ones that together operate more than a dozen fully equipped sound stages as well as one of the largest special effects stages in North America. And the business keeps growing—almost two hundred productions were shot in British Columbia in 1999. In recent years at any given time there are about two dozen projects being shot in southern British Columbia, including (predominantly American) feature movies (*Snow Falling on Cedars, Mission to Mars*); American and Canadian television movies, series, and shows (*The X-Files, Dark Angel*); and cable projects.

British Columbia's growing film industry is a major contributor to the regional economy. In 2000 alone, filmmakers spent almost 2 billion dollars on film and television productions in British Columbia. Film directly employs more than ten thousand people, while the indirect effects on the economy, from the jobs it generates in construction and tourism, for example, are even greater. Both the provincial and the federal governments recognize the value of the film industry, and in recent years they have used tax incentives and subsidies to support fledgling companies and attract new business. In 1996 film industry writer Victoria Bushnell noted, "The B.C. Film Commission has made a concerted effort to make the province appealing to out-of-towners. And Canadian unions, after resolving a number of labor conflicts last year, are arguably more supportive than some of their U.S. counterparts. Add to that the opportunity to shoot in an idyllic city in the middle of a rain forest, and who could say no?"[17]

As Bushnell points out, an important part of the attraction for the film industry is British Columbia itself. Its diversity of geography and climate offer the opportunity to shoot almost any type of outdoor scene, from the rugged wilderness needed for westerns (*McCabe and Mrs. Miller*) and adventure movies (from 1941's *49th Parallel* to the recent *Lake Placid*) to the urban settings of dramas (*Intersection*) and romantic comedies. Vancouver's core downtown with its skyscrapers and crowded streets is generic enough to substitute for Seattle (where the cost of filming can be much higher), while its attractive waterfront and diverse neighborhoods can also allow it to be a distinctive setting in its own right.

■ *Actress Gillian Anderson, star of the television show* The X-Files, *smiles on the show's Vancouver set.*

A Center for the Performing Arts

As the center for a thriving film industry and the home to many actors and actresses, perhaps it is no surprise that the province also boasts an active theater scene. Dozens of cities in British Columbia host performing companies, including Nanaimo, Burnaby, and Prince George. Theater BC, a parent organization of community theater in the province, lists almost one hundred performing arts companies. Greater Vancouver alone contains at least a dozen companies and three major theaters (the Queen Elizabeth Theatre, Vancouver Playhouse, and the Orpheum). One of the most respected companies is the Playhouse Theatre Company, which began in 1962 and each year puts on a series of five plays, by writers ranging from Henrik Ibsen to Steve Martin, as well as a few experimental works and readings. One of the unique aspects of the Playhouse Theatre Company is that it prefers to import directors to its productions rather than importing the actors from other areas. The theater believes in drawing actors from its resident players and giving local actors a chance to perform in its productions. Often the Playhouse will obtain actors from its own theater school.

In addition to the acting community, other performing arts such as music also thrive in the province. The Vancouver Symphony is the largest art organization west of Ontario and the third largest symphony in Canada. The symphony performs 140 concerts annually in the historic Orpheum, one of the largest concert halls in Canada. In addition to the Vancouver Symphony, the Victoria Symphony is a prominent and well-supported ensemble. It specializes in traveling to smaller communities in the province, thereby bringing music to people that may not be able to travel to the larger cities.

■ *Filmmakers are drawn to British Columbia's urban areas. Here, actors take a break on a Vancouver movie set.*

Provincial Support for the Arts

Arts organizations largely rely on foundations, corporations, and individuals for support. British Columbia is striving to become an additional resource for artists to turn to. The province sees its role as helping to nurture its cultural heritage and to promote artists' freedom of expression. "Culture creates the only truly lasting record of our society and its aspirations. Through culture, we grow in understanding of ourselves and our fellow British Columbians,"[18] notes the British Columbia Cultural Services Branch.

The Cultural Services Branch is a recent creation of the provincial government. The branch seeks to promote the arts not strictly as entertainment, but for their potential to unite communities and cultures. The branch has thus been able to help provide funding to book publishers, musicians, and filmmakers. The Cultural Services Branch supports artists by adhering to six goals for the arts and cultural communities: innovation and creation; artist training; production; distribution; community development; and equal access.

Museums and Galleries

Just as the provincial government provides support for the performing arts, so too does it support art and culture by directly funding museums and art galleries. Among the most prominent museums in the province is the Museum of Anthropology at the University of British Columbia in Vancouver. Since opening in 1949, the Museum of Anthropology has become a major force in educating people about the achievements and histories of British Columbia and its aboriginal peoples. The museum's collection contains First Nations objects such as totem poles, sculptures, Haida houses, feast dishes, canoes, masks, and jewelry. It also contains items from other cultures, including European ceramics, Greek and Roman artifacts, and Asian arts. At the heart of the museum, in its center rotunda, is the sculpture "Raven and the First Men" by Bill Reid, a contemporary Haida artist. The sculpture is carved out of cedar and weighs more than four tons. It depicts a raven sitting on top of a clamshell from which human figures struggle to emerge.

Even the museum's design is meant to evoke its dedication to native cultures. The noted architect Arthur Erickson designed the massive post-and-beam structure in a style that is representative of the traditional homes of the Kwakwaka'wakw people. Erickson designed the ceilings of the Great

■ *The cedar sculpture "Raven and the First Men," carved by Haida artist Bill Reid.*

Hall to be fifty feet high to allow for the museum's massive totems.

The Royal British Columbia Museum in Victoria also features a striking First Nations object as a centerpiece of its permanent collection. The First Peoples' Gallery houses a full-size re-creation of the plankhouse of Chief Kwakwabalasami. The museum also exhibits various artifacts from early Pacific Northwest coast life and a collection of striking nineteenth-century totems. The Royal British Columbia Museum also contains the re-created three-masted sloop *The Discovery*, which was Captain Vancouver's ship.

Sports and Recreation

Sports and recreation are partly determined by British Columbia's setting. Mountains make it a skier's paradise, winter sports like hockey are very popular, and the many coastal

■ A Ship with Wanderlust

Vancouver's Maritime Museum has a range of interesting exhibits, from pirate artifacts to ship models. Among its most popular attractions, however, is not a ship model but a real ship: the *St. Roch*, a 104-foot (32-meter), 323-ton schooner. (A schooner is a two-masted ship.) Launched in 1928, the *St. Roch* served as a supply ship and a floating detachment in the Arctic for the Royal Canadian Mounted Police Force. In 1940, with war underway in Europe, the Canadian government decided to use the ship to demonstrate national power and presence in the Arctic. Leaving from Vancouver to voyage through the Northwest Passage, it took the *St. Roch* twenty-seven months to reach Halifax in Nova Scotia. The *St. Roch* thus became the second ship (after the *Gjöa* in 1903–1906, commanded by the Norwegian explorer Roald Amundsen) to navigate the Northwest Passage, and the first to do it in a west-to-east direction. Two years later the *St. Roch* returned to Vancouver through a slightly more northerly route of the Northwest Passage. This eighty-six-day return journey meant that the *St. Roch* was the first ship to navigate the passage in both directions.

In a final distinction, the *St. Roch* became the first vessel to circumnavigate (journey around) North America. It accomplished this in 1950 when it traveled south from Vancouver, through the Panama Canal, and up the coast of North America to Halifax.

The *St. Roch* returned to Vancouver in 1954 and was retired four years later. In 1966 Parks Canada restored the ship to her 1944 appearance and found her a permanent indoor home in the Vancouver Maritime Museum. Self-guided tours allow visitors to imagine what life in its stark quarters must have been like for months at a time in the chilly Arctic.

areas mean boating and fishing
are year-round options. And for
those who like to watch as well as
play, Vancouver supports a number of top-tier professional sports
teams. These include the Lions
of the Canadian Football League,
the Whitecaps of the United Soc-
cer League, and the Vancouver
Canucks of the National Hockey
League. The Vancouver Grizzlies
started as a new franchise of the
National Basketball Association in
1995 but, to the disappointment
of many British Columbia basketball fans, were moved to Memphis
after the 2000–2001 season.

A downhill skier
enjoys the unparalleled
conditions of Whistler.

Not surprisingly given its mountainous location, British Columbia
offers some of the finest skiing and snowboarding in North
America, and even attracts enthusiasts from Europe, Aus-
tralia, Japan, and elsewhere. A score of top resorts dot the
province, mostly in the Coast Mountains or the Rocky ranges
in the southern section of the province. The most popular is
Whistler Blackcomb, which is located just 75 miles (120 kilometers) northeast of Vancouver. Many Vancouver residents
look forward during the winter—and other seasons—to leaving for Whistler, either by driving the picturesque Sea-to-Sky
Highway or by taking one of the regular trains. Whistler Blackcomb boasts the greatest vertical drop in North America (over
7,000 feet or 2,130 meters) and one run that's almost 8 miles
(13 kilometers) long! The pedestrian-only village at the base
of the mountain offers charming streets and vibrant nightlife.

From the heights of Grouse Mountain ski resort, another
popular area even closer to Vancouver, skiers peering down
the slope in the early spring may spy a water-skier or para-
sailor in the nearby coastal waters. Given British Columbia's
mainland and island coastline of over 16,000 miles (25,750
kilometers), it is no surprise that boating and sport fishing are
immensely popular recreational activities. In fact, Vancouver
has the largest concentration of pleasure craft in Canada. Sail-
boats, yachts, motorboats, and fishing boats all ply the waters
of British Columbia.

The sporting scene in British Columbia also includes
some unusual winter sports, such as curling. In this ancient
sport played on an ice court, teams of four players slide a 40-
pound (18-kilogram) round stone to a target area some 40

■ British Columbia's Own Cam Neely

The National Hockey League's Vancouver Canucks could hardly be accused of hometown favoritism when they traded promising twenty-one-year-old forward Cam Neely to the Boston Bruins in 1986. As it turned out, the Canucks might better be accused of stupidity, since Neely, who was born in Comox, B.C., went on to become one of the highest-scoring stars of the league over the next decade, while the player the Canucks received in return had only a few decent seasons.

Neely wasted no time showing Vancouver they'd made a mistake in dealing him, scoring a solid 36 goals in his first year as a Bruin. His bruising style and deft touch made him a threat to score whenever he had the puck. Over the next ten seasons, he had three 50-goal seasons for the Bruins and became the heart and soul of the team. In 1993 he became the second quickest, after hockey superstar Wayne Gretzky, to score 50 goals in a season, netting number 50 in only his 44th game. By the end of Neely's injury-shortened career in 1996, he had averaged almost a point (goals and assists) a game.

Today Neely is still remembered fondly in British Columbia as a great hockey player that got away. He's also held in high regard in both Boston and British Columbia as a concerned humanitarian who has done impressive charitable work. After losing both of his parents, Marlene and Michael

yards (37 meters) away. One teammate gives the stone its initial push, while two others run alongside with brooms, brushing the path of the stone so that it curls to just the right spot. Curling originated in Scotland but Canada has become a major power in the sport, with British Columbia accounting for most of the top players. In 2000, foursomes from British Columbia captured not only the men's and women's world championships, held in Glasgow, but also the men's world junior title.

Another unusual sport that has thrived in tree-covered British Columbia is lumberjacking. Expert loggers compete in various skills that loggers have traditionally used in the woods. For example, the double-

■ *A British Columbian curler watches his stone as his teammates sweep its path.*

Neely, to cancer, Cam and his three siblings began the non-profit Neely Foundation. "We know how devastating cancer is on both the patient and the family," Neely has said. "The experience left us with a deep understanding of cancer's toll on families and how much support they need to help loved ones through treatment." The foundation's most notable project is the Neely House, a first-of-its-kind bed and breakfast style home in Boston that provides shelter as well as support services for families of both adult and pediatric patients undergoing cancer treatment.

■ *British Columbian Cam Neely of the Boston Bruins scores a goal.*

bucking contest pits two-person teams to see which can most quickly saw through a twenty-inch-diameter log using a double-crosscut saw. The winning time may be less than ten seconds! Professional lumberjacks also compete in axe throwing, tree climbing, and birling (logrolling). Although such skills are not much used in today's mechanized lumber operations, the competitions link British Columbians to their forest heritage. Lumberjacks from British Columbia are top stars on the professional circuit, and the annual competition in Vancouver's Pacific National Exhibition draws thousands of enthusiastic fans.

British Columbia's young people in particular have also embraced many of the adventure wilderness sports available in the mountains and rivers, including whitewater kayaking, mountaineering, ice climbing, and heli-skiing. British Columbia youths have also been among the vanguard of those willing to try the new adrenaline-pumping "x-sports" such as ski acrobatics and bungee jumping. A site south of Nanaimo on Vancouver Island is the only bridge in North America where it's legal to bungee jump. Those who have been-there-done-that may want to ride the nearby zip line that speeds through a narrow canyon

■ *One of the many beautiful waterfalls in Yoho National Park.*

at speeds in excess of 60 miles (100 kilometers) per hour. From jet boating to rock climbing, there's plenty in British Columbia to satisfy thrillseekers who are willing to take a risk in exchange for a brief but intense rush.

A Province of Parks

British Columbia's surprising range of landscapes and climates, from wilderness glaciers to its "pocket desert," provides year-round opportunities for outdoor activities. Both the federal and provincial governments have been active in preserving wilderness areas and creating parks. These now draw a steady stream of visitors, including not only provincial residents but tourists from other parts of Canada, the United States, and overseas. British Columbia's wilderness areas offer the opportunity for hiking, backpacking, mountain biking, bird watching, trail riding, hunting, fishing, and dozens of other activities. In all, the province contains 5 national parks and 365 provincial parks totaling some 11 million acres.

The stretch of Rocky Mountain parks between Yoho National Park and Mt. Robson Provincial Park in southeastern British Columbia, along its border with Alberta, is world famous for its breathtaking scenery and rugged geography.

■ Cool Kootenay

Designated in 1920 as Canada's second national park, Kootenay (named for the Kutenai tribe) in southeast British Columbia encompasses a river valley bisected by a 58-mile (93-kilometer) parkway. Around 1915 British Columbia undertook to build the roadway as an orchard produce route. When the provincial government ran out of money for the project, the federal government stepped in and finished the road with the stipulation that five miles on either side of it would become a national park. In this case the province's early money woes led to the protection of a wonderful range of habitats between the Kootenay Mountains (a range of the Rockies) and the Rocky Mountain Trench. The adventuresome can join the mountain goats and attempt to climb 10,125-foot (3,086-meter) Mt. Verendrye, while the less ambitious can wander trails that go through conifer forests, follow the base of a 3,300-foot (1,000-meter) limestone cliff, or traverse lowland meadows with hot springs and cacti.

■ *Majestic trees and mountains are just a part of Kootenay National Park's spectacular scenery.*

"Yoho" is derived from a Cree word meaning "awe," and "yohostruck" is the usual reaction of visitors to this land of icefield-fed waterfalls, 10,000-foot (3,000-meter) peaks, and alpine meadows. The park's mile-high Kicking Horse Pass is where the Canadian Pacific Railway edged through the Continental Divide in the early 1880s, and the area still fascinates for its long tunnels and canyon-side road- and railbeds. A few miles to the east of Yoho, inside Alberta, the 140-mile (225-kilometer) Icefields Parkway drive from Lake Louise to Jasper is one of the most scenic highways in the world, with snow-glazed granite peaks rising from the shores of azure lakes.

The Rockies hold some of British Columbia's most famous parks but British Columbia's many provincial parks are treasured by locals and savvy visitors. For example, Vancouver Island's Strathcona, the oldest provincial park (designated in 1911), is a rugged wilderness with high mountain peaks that remain snowcapped year-round. It's also the site of thundering Della Falls, at 1,444 feet (440 meters) one of the highest waterfalls in Canada. Far more remote than Strathcona is Mount Edziza Provincial Park in northwestern British Columbia. It provides a dramatic reminder of British Columbia's location on the Pacific "ring of fire" volcano zone. Mount Edziza itself is a 9,144-foot (2,787-meter) -high dormant volcano that last erupted 10,000 years ago. Smaller cones, some formed as recently as 1,300 years ago, dot the volcanic landscape, along with lava flows and cinder fields. With no roads in Edziza or even *to* it, and no facilities, this park is as wild as they come.

A Rich Diversity of Attractions

British Columbia's arts and culture have developed from a lively mix of people and places. Artists and entertainers have drawn inspiration not only from the many First Nations' traditions but also from the heritage of European, Asian, and other societies that have long called the area home. In addition, the abundant natural beauty serves as an artistic inspiration as well as the setting for a diverse array of recreational and educational activities. Such attractions lead many to consider British Columbia a paradise, but the province faces numerous problems to overcome as it grows and modernizes.

Challenges Facing Contemporary British Columbia

T he people of British Columbia have always been tough and resilient. Today, however, they face a number of challenges that will test their mettle in the years to come. One important issue that is hotly debated in British Columbia today is how to balance economic growth and resource use with the need to protect the environment. Natural resources such as lumber, hydroelectric power, and fishing have helped the province grow, but these now face increasing competition from other industries such as recreation and ecotourism.

Another current challenge relates to making British Columbia's increasingly multicultural society a place where diverse peoples are able to grow and prosper. The First Nations groups whose presence in the province predates European settlement by thousands of years have become more vocal in recent years about sharing in the province's prosperity. British Columbia is also struggling to more fully accommodate its many immigrant groups, ranging from the Chinese who first came more than a century ago to the recent influx of businesspeople from Hong Kong. Many of these Asian immigrants—at first welcomed for their labor and industriousness only then to be resented and discriminated against for most of the first half of the twentieth century—have lately felt more at home in the province. Prejudice remains, however, and many obstacles are yet to be overcome. Today, British Columbia is facing the challenges of repaying the debt it owes to minority groups and making its province a more welcome home for people of all heritages.

Controversies over Lumbering Practices

British Columbia has long depended on its natural resources to fuel its economy, but how to exploit those resources while balancing jobs, provincial revenue, and environmental concerns has required imagination and a willingness to compromise. In particular, logging affects a huge portion of British Columbia, not only in the remote interior but also in the coastal rain forests. Much of British Columbia's forestland is controlled by the provincial government, due to an agreement made with Canada when British Columbia became a province. Officials in Victoria, therefore, set the rules that determine how much lumber is cut, in which parts of the province's forests, and by what methods (clear-cutting whole sections of forest, for example, or more selective culling of individual trees). The province also regulates how the harvest is to be sustained over the long term, such as by the replanting of trees. The province makes money by selling lumber companies the right to harvest trees and process logs. (A few huge international companies, such as Washington State-based Weyerhaeuser, have come to dominate the lumber industry.) Canada relies on British Columbia for approximately 40 percent of its annual lumber harvest, much of it for export to the United States and other countries.

■ *The provincial government regulates the number of trees harvested by loggers. Here, a truck is loaded with timber at a logging camp on Vancouver Island.*

In recent years, many environmentalists and some First Nations groups have grown troubled over the fate of British Columbia's public forests. Among their concerns is that the trees being replanted by the logging industry do not grow at a sufficient rate to replenish the large amounts of lumber being removed. Environmentalists also question the ongoing logging of pristine rain forests, the dense, mostly coastal forests of huge redwoods and other trees. These "old-growth" trees are especially profitable to the logging companies because of their size and the quality of the wood, but environmentalists contend that the rain forests are unique and should be preserved intact.

■ *A Vancouver Island paper mill. Environmentalists are concerned that some mills produce too much waste.*

Another area of concern relates to mill waste and how lumber is processed. When different types of mills, such as pulp mills, lumber mills, and plywood mills, work independently of each other, there is massive waste. In addition, British Columbia's logging companies often ship whole trees out of the province to foreign mills for processing. Both waste and minimal processing rob the province of potential jobs and forestry-related revenues. Thus, compared to the timber companies in California and the Pacific Northwest of the United States, British Columbia creates only one-fifth as many logging jobs per cubic yard of timber logged. The timber that is processed in British Columbia is often cut into "dimensional lumber," such as two-by-fours, and pulp (for paper such as newsprint) that also provides relatively few jobs and low revenue.

How trees are harvested also remains controversial. The clear-cuts that lumber companies favor for being the quickest and cheapest way to harvest trees can create a number of problems. Even with immediate replanting the area may take decades to fully recover. Heavy rains can erode the cleared land and cause mudslides that wash topsoil away. These mudslides prevent new plants from growing back and often damage the ecosystem of nearby salmon streams. When whole swaths of trees are destroyed, animals, birds, and insects lose not only their shelter but in some cases their food supply as well. Biologists have found that the isolated patches of trees left behind are often not able to support diverse wildlife.

Despite these concerns, few people in British Columbia want to end all logging. Many, however, are calling for reforms in current practices. As one environmentalist has noted, "It's the pace, scale, and waste of indiscriminate logging that we have been fighting. Who would think of tearing down the Tower of London as a make-work project?"[19] Fortunately, a number of new ideas and innovations have begun to provide solutions to the lumbering controversies.

New Ideas for Sustainable Logging

Public protest of clear-cutting and other questionable logging practices increased sharply in British Columbia over the past decade. One of the most prominent conflicts occurred in the early 1990s, in response to lumber companies' efforts to clear-cut rain forest valleys of the Clayoquot Sound on the west coast of Vancouver Island. Citizens from all over the province and Canada rallied to support an onsite blockade of the logging operation. The protest lasted for months and eventually led to nine hundred protesters being arrested. In 1993 the government of British Columbia issued a land-use decision that substantially reduced the area that could be logged.

Another incident occurred in the Elaho Valley north of Vancouver in 1999. A group of almost one hundred logging company workers and their friends, some using logging company trucks, traveled to the camp of local environmentalists for a vigilante-like attack. The loggers vandalized the camp

■ *Canadians protest clear-cutting in Clayoquot Sound.*

and assaulted a number of environmentalists, putting three victims in the hospital. Five logging company workers were charged with assault.

Troubling confrontations like those at Clayoquot Sound and Elaho Valley have served as a warning both to lumber companies and to the government of British Columbia that forestry reforms are desperately needed. Among the most promising alternatives to conventional logging are such practices as variable retention forestry and heli-logging. Variable retention forestry was developed by a British Columbia logging company (since sold to Weyerhaeuser) for use in old-growth natural forests like the coastal rain forests. Trees are selectively rather then clear-cut, with many trees left standing to support the local biodiversity. In some cases individual trees are trimmed while standing and then cut at the base and wedged in an upright position. Powerful helicopters are then used to grab the tree from the top and remove it with little damage to the surrounding forest.

Logging companies have also recently begun to address issues relating to waste and jobs. Mills have begun to coordinate the use of rejected or unusable parts. This new practice aids the economy both because the logging industry can make twice the product from the same amount of trees and because new employment opportunities are created within the industry.

The provincial government has also taken steps to promote greater environmental awareness among logging companies. For example, the Green Economy Secretariat, established in 2001, encourages logging companies to develop "corporate social responsibility" commitments. As the secretariat reports, "Eighty-four percent of British Columbians say they would be

■ *A clear-cut forest in British Columbia. Protests over clear-cutting have prompted timber industry changes.*

■ Birthplace of Greenpeace

Given the respect that the people of British Columbia have long paid the land, it should come as no surprise that the province has been the birthplace of numerous environmental groups and charities. Chief among these is Greenpeace, an organization that has grown to be one of the largest—and arguably most effective—nonprofit environmental groups in the world.

Greenpeace began in the early 1970s in Vancouver as part of the protest against U.S. testing of nuclear weapons in the Aleutians. Members of a group called "Don't Make a Wave" (a plea for the United States not to create a tidal wave from the atomic tests) changed the group's name to Greenpeace, shorthand for a green and peaceful world. Its organizers soon developed a unique approach that combined public protest, nonviolent direct action, political lobbying, and press-friendly fact sheets and newsletters. The effectiveness of Greenpeace's strategy was illustrated in 1971 when a few members chartered a fishing boat to enter the zone in which the United States planned to conduct nuclear tests. The test was delayed and then eventually carried out, but the United States shortly chose to terminate the remainder of the program due to the protests from Greenpeace and other groups. The site of the testing, the small island of Amchitka, is now a bird sanctuary.

Greenpeace's concerns soon ranged to include such issues as logging, the loss of the ozone layer in the atmosphere, and endangered species such as the blue whale. At the time, blues and other types of whales were being hunted to near extinction by Russian and Japanese whaling fleets. The International Whaling Commission seemed powerless to stop the huge fleets. In the summer of 1975, two Greenpeace vessels left Vancouver to find and stop whale hunters. Nearly two months elapsed before one of the Green-

more likely to purchase a product or service from a company which is socially responsible."[20]

The provincial Ministry of Forests is also beginning to take a direct role in limiting logging. In April 2001 the government of British Columbia announced support for a historic conservation agreement among environmentalists, First Nations, small rural communities, and logging companies. The plan is one of the largest conservation measures ever implemented in North America. It protects key ecological areas and promotes new approaches to conservation and forest management in the extensive Great Bear Rainforest on the Pacific coast, ranging from the northern tip of Vancouver Island to the Alaska border. The action by the government of British Columbia prohibited or deferred logging on some 3.5 million acres of Great Bear, an area four times the size of Rhode Island.

Because the logging industry is a prominent revenue source for the province, how best to operate it remains a major chal-

peace vessels discovered a Russian ship off the California coast. The Greenpeace protesters loaded themselves into small rubber dinghies and tried to get between the Russian boat and the whale they were hunting. The Russians, however, would not be kept from their prize and launched a harpoon over the heads of the protesters, killing the whale. Greenpeace captured the dramatic event on film and when it was shown it created a worldwide uproar. (Some years later similar footage released by Greenpeace showing seal hunters clubbing seals to death for their pelts began a national campaign to stop their slaughter as well.) It was not long before millions of people were calling for efforts to "save the whales," and in recent years these efforts have paid off with stricter international controls on commercial whaling.

Greenpeace continues to fight for the environment in British Columbia and around the world. It now has offices in more than thirty countries and is almost 3 million members strong. It remains an active force for environmental concern in its birthplace of British Columbia, where it has become an outspoken advocate for limiting logging in the ancient coastal rain forests.

■ *A giant inflatable whale advertises Greenpeace's "Save the Whales" slogan during a 1979 demonstration.*

lenge. But logging is no longer the dominant industry it once was. As philosophy professor T.M. Powers has noted, "Our natural landscapes no longer generate new jobs and incomes primarily by being warehouses from which loggers . . . extract commercial products. In today's world, these landscapes often may generate more new jobs and income by providing the natural-resource amenities—water and air quality, recreational opportunities, scenic beauty and the fish and wildlife—that make the Pacific Northwest an attractive place to live, work, and do business."[21]

The First Nations Seek Respect

Logging issues have been of particular concern to First Nations people, since it is their ancestral lands that in many cases are targeted by lumber companies. But the concerns of native groups are more wide ranging today, and in some cases pose a direct challenge to British Columbia's image as a successful multicultural society. Native peoples have achieved much in recent years, but many argue that the most important steps—to true independence and self-reliance—are yet to be taken. And even if many Canadians are ready to agree in principle with natives' right to self-government, tough questions still remain: What lands are each First Nations group entitled to? If private property must be purchased to create tribal homelands, where would that money come from?

For many years, the government of British Columbia resisted First Nations' efforts toward self-government and contended that their claims to ancestral lands were too ambiguous. Despite many efforts to resolve disagreements between both the provincial and federal governments and aboriginal peoples, official reform has been slow. First Nations' hopes soared in 1992 when the Charlottetown Accord was proposed. The accord included, among other items, wording that committed Canada to establishing self-government for the First Nations. As then–prime minister Brian Mulroney said, "For the aboriginal people, it proposes a new partnership in a federation that was created in 1867 without their participation. This generation of Canadians are now called upon to redeem the promises of equality first made to the aboriginal peoples several hundred years ago by representatives of French and English kings and never fulfilled. We propose to fulfil those obligations in the year 1992." In a national referendum, however, six of ten provinces (including British Columbia) rejected the accord and it never became law.

Where provincial and federal governments feared to tread, however, Canada's courts have begun to step in. In 1997, a lawsuit on the question of whether oral histories could be used as the basis for land claims went all the way to Canada's Supreme Court. In the so-called *Delgamuukw* ruling that shocked many Canadians, the Court ruled in favor of native land claims. This decision immediately awarded 22,000 square miles (57,000 square kilometers) of ancestral land to two native groups in British Columbia. It also opened the door for many similar claims and prompted provincial governments to take a more active role in resolving First Nations' land disputes. For example, an August 1998 agreement between Ottawa, British Columbia, and the Nisga'a people returned 775 square miles (2,000 square kilometers) of land in northern British Columbia to a First Nations group.

These landmark victories for the First Nations people of British Columbia have been the source of considerable uncertainty among the province's nonnative residents. Many fear that if the more than fifty ongoing First Nations' land negotiations have similar outcomes, there might not be any land left for nonnatives. In some places, native land claims have caused local real estate prices to plummet, leading to open anger between neighboring natives and nonnatives.

Despite the struggles that native Canadians are still facing, many nonnative people of British Columbia seem recently to have experienced a rediscovery of Indian culture and heritage. Young people learn more about native culture in schools and their parents pursue interests in First Nations arts and crafts. This revival of interest in native affairs seems likely to continue as political and social issues remain in the public spotlight.

■ *Nisga'a and Canadian officials celebrate the signing of the Nisga'a treaty on August 4, 1998.*

Asian Canadians

British Columbia is currently working toward making itself a color-blind province that does not tolerate discrimination. But unfortunately for Asian Canadians, this has not always been the case. Like the people of the First Nations, Asian Canadians were often expected to assimilate to the ways of Euro-Canadian life or run the risk of being discriminated against. Children were expected to go to Canadian schools and learn English and were punished for not doing so.

During World War II, after Canada joined in the war against Japan, the federal government considered Japanese Canadians to be a security risk and placed more than twenty-one thousand of them in internment (prison) camps. The majority of these men, women, and children were either naturalized citizens or Canadian by birth. Most were removed from Vancouver and coastal areas of British Columbia and relocated to camps in the country's interior. Moreover, the government seized and eventually sold off these citizens' lands and properties, presumably to pay for the costs of relocation. (In this and other respects, Japanese Canadians were treated even worse than the United States treated its own interned Japanese Americans.) Only recently, with the signing of the Japanese Canadian Redress Agreement of 1988, were many of these Asian Canadians compensated for the jobs, homes, and businesses lost due to the internment.

■ *Young immigrants
from Hong Kong line
up for class in their
Vancouver school.*

Japanese internment during World War II represented a low point for Asian Canadians in British Columbia. Although significant anti-Asian prejudice lingered into the 1950s, in recent years more enlightened attitudes have begun to prevail. In 1947, there were over fifty thousand Asians in British Columbia; today Asians make up 15 percent of the population. The steady influx into British Columbia of immigrants from the war-torn countries of Vietnam and Cambodia since the 1970s has added to the mix.

Vancouver, and British Columbia in general, has always had a high Asian population, and understandably so, as the distance between British Columbia and the Asian continent is shorter than the trip from British Columbia to the eastern provinces of Canada. Today, almost one-third of the residents of Vancouver are members of a "visible minority." Of that number, the majority is of Asian descent. Asian Canadians in British Columbia have been the cause of a quiet "cultural revolution" in the province, changing its foods, language, dress, and other traits in many ways.

Latest Wave of Chinese Immigration

On June 30, 1997, Britain's ninety-nine-year lease over its colony of Hong Kong expired and mainland China took control of the small but wealthy land. Both before and after this date, many Hong Kong residents left the country in fear of the consequences of Chinese Communist rule. For the most part, Hong Kong's loss has been British Columbia's gain.

Chinese emigrants from Hong Kong were attracted to British Columbia, and especially to Vancouver and its suburbs, for a number of reasons. No doubt many Chinese were aware of Vancouver's reputation as a beautiful city with a moderate climate and a high ranking for quality of life. Chinese emigrants also knew that Vancouver already hosts a vibrant Chinese Canadian society. Today, as many as 30,000 Asian immigrants arrive in Vancouver each year, with perhaps one-third coming from Hong Kong since the mid-1990s. The Vancouver area now has the highest concentration of Chinese people in any metropolitan area of North America. (A few cities, such as New York, San Francisco, and Toronto, have higher absolute numbers of Chinese North Americans, but Vancouver's 300,000 Chinese make up some 16 percent of the area's population, and 28 percent of the city of Vancouver.)

Another attraction for the Chinese was Canada's reputation for being a multicultural society. According to writer Marc Star, compared to the United States, "Canada is more honestly multicultural. It eschews the somewhat dishonest melting pot metaphor in favor of the more apt salad bowl. Each citizen is free—even encouraged—to retain his unique heritage, and Canada embraces them all. That's why many otherwise qualified Asian immigrants, especially those from the sister British commonwealth state of Hong Kong, forego the quest for the elusive U.S. immigrant visa in favor of Canada's open arms."[22]

The Hong Kong influx was accomplished with few of the disruptions common with large movements of peoples. But disputes did arise. For example, European Canadians complained when Vancouver-area shopping malls became so thoroughly Chinese that signs were printed only in Chinese. Longtime residents of Vancouver also voiced the opinion that

■ *Percussionists play at a New Year's celebration parade through Vancouver's Chinatown.*

■ Hong Kong's New B.C. Suburb

The recent influx of emigrants from Hong Kong affected not only the city of Vancouver but also such suburbs as Richmond. In fact, the concentration of Chinese Canadians in these suburbs now is higher than in Vancouver itself—Chinese North Americans constitute a whopping 34 percent of Richmond's population. Many of the new arrivals were successful and wealthy entrepreneurs, with a significant percentage being millionaires. They wanted, and could afford, the luxury homes and top schools found in the suburb. Since their arrival in Richmond they have set up shopping centers, opened elite restaurants, and established new businesses. The many Chinese-flavored malls in Richmond serve as a magnet for Vancouver's Chinese residents, drawing thousands into the suburb each weekend for shopping, movies, and dining.

some Asians drove in a manner more appropriate to the helter-skelter traffic patterns of Asian cities than Vancouver. Cultural differences also existed within the Asian community. For example, Chinese Canadians who had lived in Canada for generations sometimes felt that immigrants failed to respect established social and economic customs. Overall, however, the new wave of Chinese immigrants seems to be adapting well to British Columbia, and vice versa.

Toward a Harmonious Future

British Columbia continues to work to become more sensitive to the cultures of its First Nations and immigrant peoples. Provincial museums, art galleries, and festivals showcase the area's diverse history, ceremonies, and traditions. The province also supports associations and societies set up to preserve, and to educate others about, the heritage and cultural histories of these groups. By teaching a new generation to appreciate and respect the multitude of cultures in the province, British Columbia hopes to alleviate past injustices and set the stage for a more harmonious future.

As British Columbia becomes a more diverse area, it will face its environmental, economic, and other challenges with the same combination of determination and independence it has shown for centuries. Although these problems are far from being solved, British Columbia has taken steps toward resolving them and enhancing life in the province for future generations of people of all kinds.

Facts About British Columbia

Government

- Form: Parliamentary system with federal and provincial levels
- Highest official: Premier, who administers provincial legislation and regulations
- Capital: Victoria
- Entered confederation: July 20, 1871 (sixth province)
- Provincial flag: Wavy blue and white horizontal lines with a setting sun topped by a crown and the Union Jack (Great Britain's flag)
- Motto: "Splendor without diminishment"

Land

- Area: 365,946 square miles (947,800 square kilometers); third-largest Canadian province, covering 9.6% of Canada's total surface area
- Boundaries: Bounded on the north by Yukon and Northwest Territories, on the east by the province of Alberta, on the south by the states of Washington, Idaho, and Montana, and on the west by the Pacific Ocean
- Bordering bodies of water: Pacific Ocean
- National parks: Yoho, Kootenay, Glacier, Mount Revelstoke, Pacific Rim, Gwaii Hanas
- Provincial parks: more than 675, including ecological reserves and wilderness areas, encompassing some 38,000 square miles (98,000 square kilometers)

- Highest point: Mt. Fairweather, 15,320 feet (4,670 meters); sixth-highest mountain in Canada
- Largest lake: Williston, approximately 680 square miles (1,760 square kilometers)
- Other major lakes: Babine, Atlin, Kootenay, Okanagan, Upper Arrow, Lower Arrow
- Longest river: Fraser, 850 miles (1,370 kilometers)
- Other major rivers: Columbia, Skeena, Kootenay, Peace, Stikine
- Largest island: Vancouver Island, approximately 12,400 square miles (32,120 square kilometers)
- Time zones: Pacific Standard Time and Mountain Standard Time
- Geographical extremes: 48°N to 60°N latitude, 114°W to 139°W longitude

Climate

- Greatest annual average precipitation: 256 inches (650 centimeters) in Henderson Lake (North American record)
- Greatest precipitation in one month: 88 inches (223 centimeters) in Swanson Bay during November 1917 (Canadian record)
- Greatest snowfall in one season: 80 feet, 3 inches (24.5 meters) in Revelstoke in 1971–1972 (Canadian record)

People

- Population: 3,907,738 (2001 census); third-highest population of provinces and territories; 13.0% of Canada's total population of 30,007,094
- Annual growth rate: 4.9% from 1996 to 2001; fourth-highest among provinces and territories
- Density: 10.7 persons per square mile, compared to Canadian national average of 7.8 (4.4 and 3.0 persons per square kilometer)
- Location: 82% urban, 18% rural
- Predominant heritages: British, French, Asian, aboriginal
- Largest ethnic groups: Chinese, German, Italian, Vietnamese, Dutch, Greek, Japanese
- Major religious groups: Catholic, Protestant, Buddhist, Muslim
- Primary languages (first learned and still understood): 75% English, 2% French, 23% other led by Chinese
- Largest metropolitan area: Vancouver, population 1,986,965, an increase of 8.5% between 1996 and 2001; third-largest metropolitan area in Canada

- Other major cities: Victoria, New Westminster, Prince Rupert, Prince George, Kamloops, Dawson Creek, Kelowna
- Life expectancy at birth, 3-year average 1995–1997: Men 76.2 years, women 81.9, total both sexes 79.0; first among provinces and territories (Canadian average: men 75.4, women 81.2)
- Infant mortality rate in 1996: 5.1 per 1,000 live births, fourth-lowest rate among provinces and territories
- Immigration 7/1/2000–6/30/2001: 39,387, 15.6% of Canadian total of 252,088; second-highest of provinces and territories
- Births 7/1/2000–6/30/2001: 40,165
- Deaths 7/1/2000–6/30/2001: 27,582
- Marriages in 1998: 21,788
- Divorces in 1998: 9,827

Plants and Animals

- Provincial bird: Steller's jay
- Provincial flower: Pacific dogwood
- Provincial tree: Western red cedar

Holidays

- National: January 1 (New Year's Day); Good Friday; Monday preceding May 25 (Victoria or Dollard Day); July 1 or, if this date falls on a Sunday, July 2 (Canada's birthday); 1st Monday of September (Labour Day); 2nd Monday of October (Thanksgiving); November 11 (Remembrance Day); December 25 (Christmas)
- Provincial: 1st Monday of August (British Columbia Day)

Economy

- Gross domestic product per capita: $26,086 in 1999, seventh among provinces and territories and 77.1% compared to U.S. average[23]
- Gross provincial product: $124.5 billion at market prices in 2000, third among the provinces and territories and 12.3% of gross national product
- Major exports: Lumber, minerals, fish, paper and pulp products
- Tourism: Cultural and recreational attractions year-round; skiing and other winter sports
- Logging: Pulp, paper, lumber
- Mining: Copper, lead, gold, silver, zinc, coal, natural gas

Notes

Introduction: Gateway to the Pacific

1. Andrew H. Malcolm, *The Canadians*. New York: St. Martin's Press, 1985.

Chapter 1: The Majestic West

2. *Government of British Columbia*, Ministry of Forests, Queen Charlotte Islands Forest District, "Description of the Islands." www.gov.bc.ca.

3. Ivan T. Sanderson, *The Continent We Live On*. New York: Random House, 1964, p. 68.

4. Sanderson, *The Continent We Live On*, p. 71.

5. Michael Ivory, *The National Geographic Traveler: Canada*. Washington, DC: National Geographic Society, 1999, p. 274.

6. *Government of British Columbia*, Ministry of Water, Land and Air Protection, "Annual Report 1998." www.gov.bc.ca.

Chapter 2: The First Nations, the First Europeans, and the Companies

7. Dorthea Calverley, "Sir Alexander Mackenzie," *The History of the Peace*. www.calverley.dawson-creek.bc.ca.

8. *BritishColumbia.com*, "History and Heritage of British Columbia." www.britishcolumbia.com.

Chapter 3: Golden Opportunities

9. Quoted in "Oregon History—Federal Interests," *Oregon Blue Book*. http://bluebook.state.or.us.

10. Eric Lucas, "Vibrant Vancouver Benefits from Its Proud Tradition of Trade," *Horizon Air*, November 2000.

Chapter 4: Life in British Columbia Today

11. Quoted in Allan Fotheringham, "They Will Never Understand," *Maclean's*, November 6, 2000.

12. Jan Morris, *O Canada*. New York: HarperCollins, 1990, p. 162.

13. Bill McRae with Shawn Blore, *Frommer's British Columbia and the Canadian Rockies*. Foster City, CA: IDG Books Worldwide, 2000, p. 421.

Chapter 5: Arts and Culture

14. *Government of British Columbia*, Cultural Services Branch, "Cultural Policy for British Columbia." www.gov.bc.ca.

15. *Group of Seven Art.com*, "Group of Seven Art Gallery Tour: Emily Carr." www.groupofsevenart.com.

16. Donald Carroll, *The Insider's Guide to Western Canada*. Edison, NJ: Hunter Publishing, 1994.

17. Victoria Bushnell, "Vancouver, the Present: Filming in British Columbia," *MovieMaker*, October 1996. www.moviemaker.com.

18. *Government of British Columbia*, Cultural Services Branch.

Chapter 6: Challenges Facing Contemporary British Columbia

19. National Geographic Society Book Division, *Canada's Incredible Coasts*. Washington, DC: National Geographic Society, 1991, p. 169.

20. *Government of British Columbia*, Eco-Efficiency, "About Corporate Social Responsibility (CSR)." www.gov.bc.ca.

21. Quoted in "Jobs and Trees: The Forest Economy in British Columbia," *Greenpeace.org*. www.greenpeace.org.

22. Marc Star, "Asian Canada," *Goldsea Features*. http://goldsea.com.

Facts About British Columbia

23. *Demographia*, "Canada: Regional Gross Domestic Product Data: 1999." www.demographia.com.

Chronology

1592   Juan de Fuca leaves Mexico to find Northwest Passage, discovers British Columbia and charts it on his maps.

1670   Charles II of England founds the Hudson's Bay Company.

1774   Juan Perez and his crew become the first Europeans to explore the coastline of British Columbia and trade with the natives.

1778   Captain James Cook discovers the Nootka Sound while seeking the Northwest Passage.

1783   The North West Company is founded and begins to explore the western territory of Canada and establish fur-trading forts.

1788   British merchants found a fort on Nootka Sound.

1789   Martinez seizes the Nootka Sound for the Spanish government and dismantles the British forts there.

1791   A small Spanish exploration party travels down the coast of the Pacific Northwest.

1792–1794   Captain George Vancouver surveys the coast and inlets of British Columbia and his charts become the first records of the territory.

1793   On July 22 Alexander Mackenzie, after having set off from Lake Athabasca, reaches the Pacific Ocean, becoming the first European to travel across Canada by land.

1805–1806   Simon Fraser discovers the river that now bears his name while following the Columbia River looking for fur routes.

1812   David Thompson explores and maps the Columbia River to its mouth.

1821   The Hudson's Bay Company and the North West Company merge.

1827   The Hudson's Bay Company establishes Fort Langley at the mouth of the Fraser River to mark its territory against the Americans.

1843   James Douglas leads a small party to the south of Vancouver Island to build a fort, which he calls Fort Victoria.

1846   A border settlement between Great Britain and the United States establishes the 49th parallel as the boundary between the countries' territories.

1849   The British government establishes a Crown colony on Vancouver Island and hands it over to the Hudson's Bay Company to promote settlement. Richard Blanshard is established as the colony's first governor, but James Douglas quickly replaces him.

1858   Gold Rush begins on Fraser River.

1858   The British Government establishes the mainland as a British Crown Colony and calls it British Columbia. James Douglas is sworn in as governor.

1861   Gold found in the Cariboo Mountains.

1862   Opening of the Panama Canal changes British Columbia's trade market drastically, cutting weeks off the sailing time to North America's east coast.

1866   Colonies of Vancouver Island and British Columbia merge into one, retaining the name British Columbia.

1866   Jack Deighton founds Gastown (present-day Vancouver).

1869   New Westminster, the capital of the mainland colony, gives way to Victoria as capital of the new united colony.

1871   On July 20 British Columbia enters confederation and becomes the sixth province in the nation of Canada.

1871   First provincial election held in British Columbia. John Foster McCreight becomes the first premier.

1871   Prominent artist Emily Carr is born.

1885   On November 7 the Canadian Pacific Railway is completed.

1885   Glacier National Park is established.

1897   Canadian government selects Burrard Inlet as the western terminus of the Canadian Pacific Railway.

1911   Yoho National Park is established.

1915   University of British Columbia opens.

1964   British Columbia and the United States sign the Columbia River Treaty to develop and export British Columbia's hydroelectric power.

2001   Government of British Columbia announces its support for the environmental proposal to protect the Great Bear Rainforest.

For Further Reading

Michael Ivory, *The National Geographic Traveler: Canada*. Washington, DC: National Geographic Society, 1999. This handsomely illustrated book explores all aspects of the province, from brief histories of the areas to details for the modern traveler including places to see, shop, and eat.

Bern Keating, *Inside Passage*. Garden City, NY: Doubleday, 1976. Photos and text describe the sights, plants, and animals along the province's stunning coastal waterway.

Andrew H. Malcolm, *The Land and People of Canada*. New York: HarperCollins, 1991. The author of the bestselling *The Canadians* presents a capsule summary of the country and its provinces.

Bill McRae with Shawn Blore, *Frommer's British Columbia and the Canadian Rockies*. Foster City, CA: IDG Books Worldwide, 2000. Very detailed and up-to-date information about all sections of the province.

National Geographic Society Book Division, *Canada's Incredible Coasts*. Washington, DC: National Geographic Society, 1991. This book offers the spectacular photos and concise, well-documented text for which the magazine is famous.

Works Consulted

Books

Hugh Brody, *Maps & Dreams*. New York: Pantheon Books, 1982. A personal account of a young anthropologist's experience with Beaver Indians of northeast British Columbia.

Donald Carroll, *The Insider's Guide to Western Canada*. Edison, NJ: Hunter Publishing, 1994. This practical and well-illustrated book offers background and traveler's information on B.C. and Canada's three other western provinces.

Andrew H. Malcolm, *The Canadians*. New York: St. Martin's Press, 1985. A personalized account (written by an American son of Canadians) of the peculiar national characteristics of both Americans and Canadians and how they contribute to a unique relationship.

Jan Morris, *O Canada*. New York: HarperCollins, 1990. An insightful cultural observer trains her eye and pen on the Canadians.

Peter C. Newman, *Empire of the Bay: The Company of Adventurers That Seized a Continent*. New York: Penguin, 1998. This is an informative tale of the formation of the Hudson's Bay Company and its impact on Canada.

Roger Riendeau, *A Brief History of Canada*. Markham, Ontario: Fitzhenry and Whiteside, 2000. An excellent history of Canada, from the first European explorations through modern times, told in a clear, easy-to-follow manner.

Ivan T. Sanderson, *The Continent We Live On*. New York: Random House, 1964. This nontechnical description of North America covers land formations, weather, and wildlife.

John Saywell, *Canada: Pathways to the Present*. Rev. ed. Toronto: Stoddart, 1999. Explores the conflicts affecting Canada's history, today's emerging solutions, and the nation's uncertain future.

Periodicals

Allan Fotheringham, "They Will Never Understand," *Maclean's*, November 6, 2000.

Eric Lucas, "Vibrant Vancouver Benefits from Its Proud Tradition of Trade," *Horizon Air*, November 2000.

Internet Sources

Victoria Bushnell, "Vancouver, the Present: Filming in British Columbia," *MovieMaker*, October 1996. www.moviemaker.com

Dorthea Calverley, "Sir Alexander Mackenzie," *The History of the Peace*. www.calverley.dawson-creek.bc.ca.

Greenpeace.org, "Jobs and Trees: The Forest Economy in British Columbia." www.greenpeace.org.

Marc Star, "Asian Canada," *Goldsea Features*. http://goldsea.com.

Websites

BritishColumbia.com (www.britishcolumbia.com). This private website covers topics such as tourism, attractions, recreation, and wildlife.

Demographia (www.demographia.com). This site offers a range of useful statistical information and market research on Canada and other countries.

Government of British Columbia (www.gov.bc.ca). The provincial website provides the latest news as well as tourist information, background facts, links to ministries, and more.

Group of Seven Art.com (www.groupofsevenart.com). This site provides bios on the noted Canadian artists as well as an extensive gallery of paintings.

Oregon Blue Book (http://bluebook.state.or.us). The official state Internet directory includes a detailed history of the Pacific Northwest.

Index

Picture Credits

Cover Credit: © Jim Richardson/CORBIS
© Annie Griffiths Belt/CORBIS, 70, 76, 94
Associated Press/Canadian Press, 93
BC Archives, 27, 32, 42, 46 (bottom), 49, 55, 58, 72
© Bettmann/CORBIS, 81
© CORBIS, 22, 54
Dan Coleman/Archive Photos, 89
© Ecoscene/CORBIS, 17
FPG International, 79, 82
© George D. Lepp/CORBIS, 26
© Gunter Marx Photography/CORBIS, 23, 51, 53, 67, 77, 83, 86, 95
© Hulton/Archive by Getty Images, 34, 35, 40, 46 (top), 75, 91
© Joel W. Rogers/CORBIS, 21, 25, 28, 61
© Kevin R. Morris/CORBIS, 66
Library of Congress, 30
© Natalie Fobes/CORBIS, 63
North Wind Picture Archives, 41
© Paul A. Souders/CORBIS, 60
PhotoDisc, 11, 14, 19, 64, 65, 69, 74, 87
© Reuters New Media Inc./CORBIS, 80
© Wolfgang Kaehler/CORBIS, 88

About the Author

Brett J. Palana is a native of Rhode Island. She currently works in the publishing industry dealing with the development and production of high school and college level textbooks. Previously, she has written and edited for several academic journals, including *MELUS*, a multiethnic literature publication. She received her bachelor's degree in English from Stonehill College in Massachusetts and holds a master's degree in the same discipline from Rhode Island College. While pursuing her master's degree she began a study of the ancient Greek language and has since translated several plays. Brett and her husband, Scott, currently live in southern Massachusetts.

LINCOLN
REGIONAL

DISCARD

CHICAGO PUBLIC LIBRARY
SULZER REGIONAL
4455 N. LINCOLN
CHICAGO, IL 60625